Matthew Silvan

A Life

That Knows

No Age

Reflections on Life's
"Golden Years"

New City Press

Published in the United States by New City Press
206 Skillman Avenue, Brooklyn, New York 11211
©1991 New City Press, New York

Translated by Anne Lingley from the original Italian edition
Una Vita Senza Età
©1989 Città Nuova Editrice, Rome, Italy

Cover design by Nick Cianfarani

Library of Congress Cataloging-in-Publication Data:

Silvan, Matteo.
    [Una vita senza età.   English]
    A life that knows no age : reflections on life's "Golden years"   /
  Matthew Silvan.
       p.   cm.
    Translation of: Una vita senza età.
    ISBN 0-911782-95-8 (pbk.) : $6.95
      1. Silvan, Matteo. 2. Catholics—Italy—Biography. I. Title.
  BX4705.S6325A3   1991
282'.092—dc20
[B]   91-23281

Printed in the United States of America

A Life

That Knows

No Age

Contents

Introduction

Third and last

The doorbell rang. It was a dear old friend of mine coming for a visit. We greeted one another warmly and made our customary inquiries. He too was a widower and this, in a certain way, had a strengthening effect on our friendship. He asked about the progress of my work. "How is it going with your book about life's 'golden years'? Did you finish it yet?"

"This is it right here," I replied, picking up a folder of papers from the table.

"So the 'saga' of your life goes on, and this is part three."

"Third and last, my friend. This book marks the end. I can hardly be expected to write the chronicle of my funeral."

He smiled and leafed through the pages. "There's no preface."

"No," I said, "I didn't think of having one. And then I wouldn't know whom to ask to prepare it. Anyway, you don't have to have one, do you? I remember when I used to practically devour books and I just skipped over the preface."

"When I was young I used to do that, too," came his reply. "But then I realized that the preface was something useful because it helped the reader to understand the book. It was like the key."

"Well forgive me for being impertinent, but that might be true if the authors can't quite explain themselves, or if they use technical language, or attempt a new literary form. I've seen, for example, the works of those writers who feel it is their duty to destroy syntax in order to produce a work of 'linguistic eversion' in harmony with the 'social eversion' they proclaim. In their books they go on for pages without periods, commas or conjunctions. Allow me to offer you a taste of this 'eversion': both social and literary."

I got up and took a folder down from the shelf. Pulling out a clipping I handed it to my friend. I had underlined the following piece: "It is not easy to knife someone it is not as easy as it might seem that is it is easy to knife someone but not to kill him because one does not just allow himself to be knifed he tries to react by avoiding the blow and he moves about and it is not too easy to hold him still and so one method is to grab him around the neck and strangle him until he has almost lost consciousness and then attempt to strike a blow. . ."

"What do you think of that?" I inquired. "It would appear from this piece that the author is a specialist in the art of killing and he's trying to teach others this art. My attempt, and I emphasize the word 'attempt,' is to capture the basics of the 'art of loving.' I try to enter into a conversation with my readers whom I love, even though I do not know them. I try to use their language, the same easy going style I would use if I were talking to them personally. The periods and commas and even the suspension points help to reproduce that same rhythm of pauses that occur in a peaceful conversation between friends. I do not hesitate to use a capital letter for words like Love, Life, Unity when I want them to denote something of the divine. I want others to understand what I mean so I try to express myself in the simplest possible way. If you only knew, my dear friend, how hard it is to write in a simple way."

He sat there somewhat perplexed, questioning me with his eyes. "Let's leave it at that" he concluded. "If that's your view on the matter I have nothing else to add. However, let me remind you that you happily accepted the preface that Igino Giordani wrote for your first book *Lazarus Come Out,* remember?"

"Of course," I replied, "I was very pleased with that. But he, that dear friend, was the one to offer such a gift. If you recall, that preface appeared only in the third edition of the book. The first two had no preface. And my second book, *Love is Stronger,* had no preface and it seems it was alright like that."

"Yes," he admitted, "I'll grant you that. The immediate

contact that you establish with your readers produces an effect. But, if you'll forgive me for insisting, in this third book of yours you're taking it for granted that the readers know who you are, what you do, where you live. This will be of no surprise to those who have read your other books, but it may leave somewhat puzzled those who, attracted by the title, take this book in hand and meet you for the first time. I think it would be good to offer this category of readers at least a little explanation."

At this point I had to concede that he was right. A preface was needed for the new readers. I hadn't thought of it. I did not know whom to ask. " But wait a minute . . . this may seem rather bold of me but if we're speaking about a presentation, why couldn't I write it. Do I have to find someone else to do it? Who knows my story better than I?"

I burst into laughter. I was laughing at myself of course. My friend, however, wasn't laughing. "You're incorrigible," he exclaimed.

The "before" and the "after"

And now, my dear "new" friends, allow me to briefly recount the events of the latter part of my life. Once you know the "before" you will better understand the "after."

My name is Matthew Silvan and I was born in 1904 in San Venanzo, a small town in the region of Italy called Umbria. I worked for many years in Rome in various departments of the Treasury and in different countries of Europe where I was sent because of my expertise in financial matters. During the war, in 1941, I was sent first to Berlin to help resolve certain economic questions and then in 1942 to Yugoslavia.

After the war, I was stationed in London and given a diplomatic status. It was 1952 and there was much work to do to settle Germany's pre-war debts. In 1954 I lived in Paris. Afterward I worked as a representative to the OECE (Organization for European Economic Cooperation) of the area referred to as the "free territory of Trieste."

Home base of course was always Rome and more precisely, the so-called "button room" of the Treasury. As I was always involved in public life, due to the delicate nature of my work, I thought it best to sign the articles I wrote at that time with pen-names. The last of them is the one I have used for this book; I have kept it even though it would be no longer necessary.

I wrote and I write in fact about the truer story of my life, the one which has much deeper significance. It began in 1954, or better, it began when I discovered, incredible but true, a gold mine! It wasn't like the gold reserve kept in the inner sanctum of Italy's Central Bank which I had the duty to inspect. Rather it was the gold that one finds only in the safes of the Most High and is known by the name God-Love.

Naturally, I immediately and avidly began digging this mine and, as if by magic, my whole way of thinking and living did a complete about-face.

This gold-mine of life is called the Work of Mary. It is an association of faithful, begun in 1943, which came to life, like a fine gem, in the heart of a young woman from Trent: Chiara Lubich. In brief, the spirituality of this gem aims at bringing about, through Love, the ardent prayer of Jesus "that all may be one" (Jn 17:21). It is centered on His promise to be there "where two or three are gathered" in His name (cf. Mt 18:20).

Concretely, then, this spirituality is lived out in the focolare centers: small, separate communities of men or women. These are persons consecrated to God, yet living like other lay people in the midst of the world. They do not flee the company of others as was once considered necessary in order to live a truly Christian life. They love and seek perfection by doing the will of God wherever circumstances bring them: in their families, at school, and at work.

I, too, became a part of this movement when I was fifty. Others in my family did as well. My family became a "Focolare family" where I lived with my wife and my two daughters. After a while our daughters left us, each to follow their own vocation: one chose to consecrate her life to God in the Focolare. Shortly afterwards she left for New York with two other companions to open the focolare centers there. The second got married and left to form a family. My wife Teresa, and I remained alone but the door of our home was always open. It remained a meeting point for the people of the Focolare community in Rome.

Suddenly, on April 18, 1977, Teresa died with the serenity of one who is well prepared for the encounter with God.

I did not fall apart or give in to despair. I went to our pastor and asked him not to have the usual sad funeral. Teresa had simply left for another place. "Please talk about the resurrection," I said. And he did so. Following that, I wrote to Chiara Lubich and told her that I did not feel like a widower, nor did I feel alone. I told her that I was ready—if she felt it was the case notwithstanding my seventy-three years—to enter one of the men's focolare centers in Rome.

The request was granted. My natural family was substituted by a supernatural family. My "superior" was forty years my junior. But life went on quite serenely.

The chapters which follow are pages of a diary written between 1980 and 1984. They express reflections and recount episodes seemingly detached from one another. But at the center of each situation is the heart of a man who lives and loves his "golden years." He loves them because he loves the One who granted them to him, through no merit of his own.

I would like to conclude this self presentation by letting the readers know that in the following pages I do not intend to discuss the complex issue of aging. Everyone is already aware of the questions that are being raised about the plight of the elderly. Should they be placed in rest homes or have at-home nursing care? Is it detrimental to move the elderly to places far from their home town? Hospitals can no longer provide beds for elderly patients or for younger ones either. Should we build complexes for the chronically ill? Should they provide single rooms or rooms with many beds? Will elderly couples be provided with suitable living quarters or will they have to live separately? And so on and so forth.

Discussions on this issue are our daily fare but, as I said, I do not intend to enter into it. I will instead offer my personal experience which I would like to link to that of Igino Giordani, guide and friend, who, at the age of eighty wrote:

> To rediscover the meaning and dynamics of existence; to gain back, amidst physical suffering . . . an ever more luminous youthfulness. . .

> Afflicted by physical ailments, in silence, in stillness (forced, but nonetheless welcome), I now attend, as best I can, the novitiate of preparation for the encounter with Love, and therefore with Life.*

The goal is a lofty one. Will I ever reach it? I will at least start out. I am certain that by the end Someone will come out to meet me and take me by the hand just as a loving mother does with her child.

---

* Igino Giordani, *Memorie d'un cristiano—Memoirs of a Christian* (Rome: Città Nuova, 1984) 164-165.

The Golden Years

To die at one hundred

At this point it might be a good idea to ask what is meant by the "golden years." When do they begin? When do they end? Opinions differ.

One precise idea on the matter—somewhat challenging I'll admit—comes from the Bible. Isaiah, at the heights of exultation for the freedom of the chosen people from the slavery in Babylonia, exclaims among other things: "Thus says the Lord . . . I create new heavens and a new earth. . . There a child will not die at an early age and neither will the one who has not yet reached the fullness of his days because the youngest will live to a hundred" (Is 65:17, 20).

Scholars say that this is a prophetic vision, a means by which the author expresses the fullness of joy. And that is certainly true. But I would like to optimistically regard this opinion as a reference point. If we divide one hundred by three, then the so-called "golden years," rounding things out a little, fall between sixty-six and ninety-nine years. This criterion seems acceptable to me also because, generally speaking, at sixty-six, more or less, one starts receiving his or her pension.

However, it is appropriate to make a distinction between those persons who are at the beginning of this period and those who are close to the end.

At the beginning of this span of time, normally speaking, one still has the strength and sharpness of mind to accept new ideas and glimpse new horizons. But, with the passing of years, one can live in peace only if one has seen to it, like the wise virgins, that there is enough oil to remain with the lamp lit until the "bridegroom" arrives.

I would like to read with you, dear readers, this parable taken from the twenty-fifth chapter of Matthew:

The kingdom of heaven shall be compared to ten maidens who took their lamps and went to meet the bridegroom. Five of them were foolish, and five were wise. For when the foolish took their lamps, they took no oil with them; but the wise took flasks of oil with their lamps.

As the bridegroom was delayed, they all slumbered and slept. But at midnight there was a cry, "Behold, the bridegroom! Come out to meet him." Then all the maidens rose and trimmed their lamps. And the foolish said to the wise, "Give us some of your oil, for our lamps are going out." But the wise replied, "Perhaps there will not be enough for us and for you; go rather to the dealers and buy for yourselves."

And while they went to buy, the bridegroom came, and those who were ready went in with him to the marriage feast; and the door was shut.

Afterward the other maidens came also, saying, "Lord, Lord, open to us." But he replied, "Truly, I say to you, I do not know you."

Watch therefore, for you know neither the day nor the hour.

It is foolish, therefore, not to prepare oneself in time for the change in life that the golden years comport.

But what exactly do we mean by "in time"? My friend Aristide, with whom I am discussing the topic, has posed this question. "It's not easy to give a precise answer," I began, "because the length of each person's life is different. But it's good to be wise . . . and I would dare to say that one should give it some careful thought right after having celebrated his or her fiftieth birthday."

"Oh no, you're exaggerating!" he exclaimed. "After fifty one is still in the prime of life!"

"Of course!" I replied. "The sun is at its apex at midday. But at 12:01 it's already on its way down."

My friend looked at me astonished. Then, with an ironic "So long," he turned and left.

The one who loves lives

My friend's abrupt departure made me pause and think. Many people, even though they lived their whole life as "good Christians," reach their senior years and are at a loss as to how to remain in the fullness of light while experiencing the gradual decline of their faculties.

I wonder why we couldn't give them the opportunity to open themselves up to divine grace and enter one of those religious communities where one can be both active and contemplative? There they could reflect in peace on the journey that still lies ahead of them.

I am referring in particular to those people who remain alone. But even those who are tied by family bonds may feel the need to firmly direct themselves toward the true life once they have understood (before or after doesn't matter) that in the world everything is vanity of vanities.

It's true that religious orders and communities, including those composed of committed lay people, more commonly accept young people as candidates. Certainly the future is in their hands. But does one's age have to be an insurmountable obstacle when at fifty, or even sixty, they possess an ardent heart?

It's also true that the "rules" of life of these institutes are at times quite severe. But for these "newcomers" a less stringent rule could be formulated to allow for varying levels of commitment: from simple participation in the spiritual life of the order to explicit consecration to God through promises.

Obviously the passing from a generic form of Christianity to a radical commitment—particularly if oriented toward entrance into one of these communities—would require an adequate period of formation: almost like a . . . novitiate.

To this end, courses in community life could be instituted focusing particularly on how to live in mutual love and share one's talents. No matter how absurd it might appear I maintain that there should be "schools" where elderly persons can learn how to live their golden years with a thorn in their heart and a smile on their lips. In fact I will never tire of repeating the one who loves lives, not the one who sits back waiting to be loved.

At this point I would like to refer to two elderly biblical characters who are quite symbolic in regard to this issue. I am referring to Simeon and Anna, the prophetess. The former took baby Jesus up in his arms when he had been brought to the temple and "blessed God and said, 'Lord, now let your servant go in peace.' "

The latter, a widow, had reached the age of eighty-four. "She," we read, "did not depart from the temple, worshipping with fasting and prayer night and day. And coming up at that very hour she gave thanks to God, and spoke of him to all who were looking for the redemption of Jerusalem" (Lk 2:28-29; 37-38).

Roses and thorns

A friend offered my companions in the focolare center and myself the use of her little house in the mountains. We decided that we would spend there, in perfect harmony, our brief vacation.

We arrived rather late in the evening and I slept soundly the whole night through. When I woke up the house was empty. A note left on the table informed me that my friends had all left on a hike to the top of one of the nearby peaks.

I swung open the window which faced out over the valley and a breath of fresh, fragrant air greeted me.

How wonderful! After days and days of rain the sun was shining brilliantly.

I looked around and everything, every little detail intrigued me. Like this flaming red rose that was reaching up to my window. What message did it bring?

The words of a song of my youth came to mind: "Love, love, bring me many roses. . ."

That was water under the bridge. My youth was gone, the love I have now is a different one, and the roses. . .

Before I knew it I was wading into the treacherous sea of memories. But I immediately caught myself and thought, "It's true, love is different now but, since it has been purified, it has acquired a much greater dimension."

"And the roses?" I asked myself.

They go on blooming, I reasoned, almost with a sigh, but this particular variety has a lot of thorns.

Ah yes, a lot of thorns. But I was not about to stop and count them, nor was I going to close myself off for fear of being injured by them. If one can say that there is no rose without a thorn, one can also say that there is no thorn without a rose.

The golden years bring a certain advantage. When one is freed from the spur of daily work and can live in communion of soul with others then it becomes easier to accept the thorns, that is, the impediments that crop up as the years pass, and share with the others the roses.

But what roses can we offer? That's simple: the great gift we can give to those who pass us by, every day or once in a while, is the smile on our face.

Many sufferings? Many smiles. Those are our roses.

That grandmother

My friends returned from their hike, tired but happy. They had reached the top of the mountain. One of them apologized for having left me alone the whole day. But I replied that in spite of being alone I hadn't been bored. "I lived a very full day indeed. I even did some writing in my diary and my concluding affirmation states that at a certain age this principle should hold true: 'Many sufferings? Many smiles!' "

I couldn't help but notice the puzzled expression on my friends' faces. I attempted an explanation.

"A smile might not seem to be worth too much and in fact if you smile just out of courtesy or out of need it's not terribly meaningful. But it has a completely different meaning if its source is a suffering that has been accepted and then transformed out of love. Then that smile can even be a source of life for someone who has lost their way."

My young friends were astonished. I thought I'd better tell them about an incident that once happened to me and that I'll never forget.

I was on a train heading for Turin as part of my job as the delegate of the Federal Reserve to the stock exchange. When we stopped in Genoa everyone got off except myself and a middle-aged woman. As is normal in these situations we began a polite conversation and before long my travelling companion began to complain that her son studied very little or not at all. I observed that yes, young people need to study, but they shouldn't necessarily be martyred for it. She agreed and, to show her support for my theory, added:

"Yes, sometimes I worry, but I try not to go overboard, especially after what happened to a friend of mine. Listen to this. One day her son, a high school student like mine, came home from school, sat down at the table as usual and then announced, 'I'm not going to eat.'

" 'Why not, are you feeling sick?'

" 'I feel fine, but I don't want to eat.'

" 'But what happened?'

" 'Nothing. I just want to die!'

"Well," the lady continued, "you can imagine the fright my friend got. She called me immediately to see if my son had told me anything. But he knew nothing; nothing unusual had happened.

"But this young man wouldn't snap out of it so my friend brought him to see a psychologist. She asked me to come with her and so I did.

"Her son offered no resistance. When we got there the doctor invited him into his study so that they could talk while we waited outside. After about an hour they came out. They didn't say a word but the doctor made a sign that there was nothing seriously wrong. Afterward he called my friend on the phone and you'll never guess what his findings were.

"It turned out that the young man was perfectly normal. He answered all the doctor's questions, his studies were going well, he had money in his pocket, he was not love-sick.

" 'So why have you upset your whole family like this?' the doctor exclaimed. 'Why do you want to die?'

" 'Because nobody loves me.'

" 'But how can you say that. Your parents have given you everything. Every year you go to the beach or the mountains on vacation. They are giving you the chance to study so that your future will be more secure. . .'

" 'Sure, they're interested in making sure that my future is secure, but right now they leave me all alone. The only person who really loved me, who took the time to smile at me was my grandmother, but now she's dead.'

"No one could believe their ears," my travelling companion continued. "His grandmother's legs were paralyzed, you know. She had lived in a wheelchair for over ten years. When she died everyone breathed a sigh of relief. I did too, I hate to admit, but after all, in her condition, she couldn't do anything for herself or, it seemed, for anyone else. And here they were telling us that she was the only one who understood that young man. She spent time with him and talked about his interests, she consoled him, listened to him, gave him advice and smiled at him. Yes, she smiled even when she had to admonish him. That paralyzed grandmother kept a sixteen-year-old youth, who was con-templating suicide, going with her smile."

A long period of silence followed. The train rumbled along. The lady herself seemed to be surprised at the conclusion she herself, perhaps unintentionally, had reached. My thoughts turned not to the youth but to the grandmother. My conclusion was a precise one: the golden years have thorns, but also roses; ailments, but also joys. That grandmother was a source of life for the young man, but at the same time she was regenerating herself.

Thus my story ended. My friends were silent. Finally someone spoke: "This is not an isolated incident. I recently read in the newspaper that a child killed herself after her grandmother died."

The others nodded. I thought to myself, "Grandmothers, always grandmothers. What are the grandfathers doing. Why can't they inspire this kind of love."

"Well, there are also some children who adore their grandfathers."

To live more

Our vacation was whizzing by. It seemed like we just got there and we were talking about leaving. I decided to take stock of how this period had gone. All in all it was like living twenty days of contemplation. Everything and everyone brought me joy: my friends with whom I shared the house and those I met outside. My every activity, even washing the dishes, was carried out in secret dialogue with the Creator and his created ones. Perhaps without my even being aware of it, Saint Francis was singing within me.

Of course I wasn't able to do everything that my younger friends did: no long hikes, no scaling the peak. Besides, I knew that those pale, barren, mountains were but the skeletons of dead giants, rocks that would inevitably wear away to nothing. It hurt to think about it. After all they were so beautiful. But alas I had to remain in the valley, alone.

I refused, however, to allow myself to be dominated by an

inferiority complex. Rather I was determined to express the fullness of my personality as a senior citizen. A person, that is, with no desire to turn back the clock, a person who knows that his life is different, yes, but equally rich in meaning.

My task was to write, collect and organize the pages of my diary. Yet there was still time every day to take a few walks, even when it was drizzling, to contemplate nature, to meditate, to chat with the local people and, at the close of each day, to attend Mass with my friends.

While walking I recited the rosary and reviewed the joyful, sorrowful and glorious mysteries of the life of Jesus and Mary. This opened up unexplored horizons for me. Those events, and the world in which they took place were, after all, the personal and historic events of each one of us pilgrims here on earth.

Every once in a while one of my young friends asked if I wanted company while saying the rosary. I would decline, regretfully, because it seemed to go by too fast when we said it in two. I, instead, preferred to say it alone, slowly, pausing often to meditate on the profound sense of each mystery. If I happened to catch myself thinking of something else while I prayed I started all over again: no shortcuts!

And then, I had a secret method for making the rosary even more alive. To each Hail Mary I linked the name of a person for whom I felt it was important to pray or for whom I had been asked to pray. And since these people are spread all over the world, I skimmed over the whole planet as I prayed. I began with Rome where the people who are dearest to me live. Then I hopped over the Atlantic to North America. From there, passing through New York, I continued on my journey: South America, Africa, the Philippines, Korea and so on. When the trip was over I returned to Europe and came to a halt in Italy.

This is easy for me during vacation time. There's no need to rush, and I can take time to think, meditate and start over. Even when I go back to the city, if I organize my time well perhaps I will still be able to make this spiritual journey every day.

The fact of having so much free time is the best asset of being a senior citizen provided, however, that it is oriented towards nourishing the values of the spirit and not towards seeking an escape from loneliness.

Reaching Tabor

The City of Mary

The days have passed and our vacation was over. Before leaving we stopped in to thank Pat, the lady who lent us her house. But she turned the tables and began thanking us for coming.

We set out for Rome but on the way I stopped off in Loppiano, a place I had wanted to visit for a while now.

Many of my readers have already heard of this little city. It is, among other things, a meeting point for hundreds of young people who aim at accomplishing the ideal of a world without barriers such as exists in the depths of every human heart. This ideal is often considered to be a utopia but in this place it is a reality.

"Loppiano," the young man who welcomed me on my arrival explained, "is the name of an old farm that was located here amidst fields and farm houses. Some families live here on a permanent basis while the young men and women—accommodated in two separate areas—come for a period of about two years. They experience a new style of life which is active and contemplative at the same time. It is a life lived while working, studying and praying. Here the barriers between races, cultures, and different age groups are overcome. As a matter of fact, such a barrier would be inconceivable."

"It's not that we think we'll be able to change the world overnight," another young man added as he drove me to the place where I would sleep. "But we would like to bear witness to the world that unity, and therefore peace, is possible. If they ask us what the motivating force behind all this is, well, we tell them openly that it is love. But not love as people commonly think of it."

The young man hesitated. He did not know that I have been active in the Focolare since before he was born. And I didn't tell him. I preferred to let him talk and I encouraged him to continue with his explanation.

"This means, therefore, that we must go beyond ourselves and our own personal ideas and make room within us for the other person. In this way there are no more divisions, for example, between me, an Italian, and that young man from Uganda who waved at us back there. One ring in a chain forming a future unity is already forged."

The young man looked at me and smiled. I smiled back. Soon we reached the house where I would be staying. Blue Field was the name of the area where this rustic house was located.

I fell into a deep sleep that lasted for about ten hours. When I awoke I ate breakfast and walked outside.

There was no one around. The young men who lived there were at school or at work. They alternate these activities because no human and religious formation can be considered complete if it doesn't include the experience of earning one's living.

I set out for a walk. All of a sudden a young pheasant crossed the road in front of me. The sun, the green, the olive trees, the song of birds near and far. What joy!

How mysterious creation is! What an infinite variety of sounds and colors form one marvelous reality.

My thoughts drifted to Assisi, to Saint Francis. I imagined the Church of San Damiano where, with his Song to all Creation, Francis had lifted up to God a sublime canticle of praise:

Praise to you, my Lord, in all your creatures,
Especially Sir Brother Sun,
Who makes the day,
and through whom you give us light.
And he is beautiful and radiant with great splendor,
and bears the signification of you, Most High.

Praise to you, my Lord, for Sister Moon and the stars,

You have formed them in heaven
clear and precious and beautiful.

Praise to you, my Lord, for Brother Wind,
And for the air—cloudy and serene—
and every kind of weather.
By which you give sustenance to your creatures.

Praise to you, my Lord, for Sister Water,
Which is very useful and humble
and precious and chaste.

Praise to you, my Lord, for Brother Fire,
By whom you illumine the night,
And he is beautiful and cheerful
and robust and strong.

The canticle goes on praising "Mother Earth," "Sister Death."
Everything, heaven and earth, life and death, led Francis to sing
praise to God.

I looked around and saw that it was really all still true. What
else could I utter except, "My God and my all."

The game of love

At noon, Mass in a large hall. A multi-racial choir of young
men sang a beautiful song. I had heard it before and it always
moved me. It spoke to me of those moments when my soul
tossed between light and shadow, between love and fear. Here
are some of its words:

Sometimes my lamp seems to falter
somehow I light it again.
Maybe in this way you tell me
that all our life is a game.

All that I treasure I give you,
riches beyond all compare.

Yet in my house there is nothing,
its rooms are empty and bare.
Nothing is all I can give you.
Nothing is all I can share.

As when the crying of children
changes to laughter again,
if I live moment by moment
I can continue your game.

I know that you'll be the winner,
loving is all I need do.
Gladly I follow your footsteps,
hoping my life you'll renew.
When by your light I am guided,
I can't but come back to you.

An inexpressible warmth came over me. The words of the liturgy that followed sounded even more rich in meaning.

There was a reading from the book of Genesis, and the gospel was followed by a brief homily. The priest's words clarified the meaning of the first reading and I was struck by something I had not thought of before.

The episode being recounted referred to Jacob who wanted to return to the land of his fathers, but while he was preparing to cross the river someone tried to stop him. Jacob, refusing to be discouraged, struggled with the unknown intruder the whole night. This other, unable to prevail, struck Jacob on the hip and then tried to get away. Unable to escape he shouted:

"Let me go, dawn is breaking!"

"I will not let you go," replied Jacob, "unless you give me your blessing."

"What is your name?" the other asked.

"Jacob . . . please tell me your name?"

"Why is it that you ask?" And he blessed him there.

Jacob had by now understood that his adversary was an angel

of God. He pretended to keep Jacob out but he desired most ardently that he pass.

"I saw the Lord face to face," Jacob then said, "and yet I live." However, together with the blessing, he had received a "sign." The blow he received on his hip would cause him to limp for the rest of his life (cf. Gn 32:24-32).

Wasn't this, Lord, a little like my story. Hadn't I one day offered God my life, even my eyes, just to be able to enter into a friendship with him? My offer, repeated now and then, seemed to fall on deaf ears. But one day, as I recounted on another occasion,* my plea was heard. The struggle lasted five months. I was victorious in the end but I had lost the use of one eye. This would be the reminder of the gift I had received.

I had often asked myself after that what part violence plays. Was Jacob violent for wanting to enter the land of his fathers at any cost, or was the Other one violent, trying to stop him?

Jesus once said: "No one can come to me unless the Father who sent me draws him" (Jn 6:44). So it is the Father who takes the initiative and it should be enough to reach the edge of the river, show your "pass" and cross to the other side.

But that's not how it is. There is a toll to pay. The passageway is so very narrow that in order to pass through you not only have to struggle but you have to be detached from everything: father, mother, possessions, and even your very life!

But what joy awaits you on the other side. What freedom! Everything is given back to you, purified. And then you realize that everything really is a game of Love.

Come and live with us

That afternoon, everyone met again for meditation. The young men were sitting on the grass outdoors, attentively listening to the person responsible for the little city. In the silence of

---

* See *Lazarus, Come Out* (New York: New City Press, 1980)

that place, his voice could be heard even by those sitting farthest away.

Once in a while my attention was drawn to the scene around me. Everything seemed to be transformed. The Sermon on the Mount probably looked something like this. Now I understand why a bishop who was visiting Loppiano talked about "reaching Tabor."

The topic of this evening's meditation is, as always, a fascinating one: the truth! Where is it? What is it?

The speaker was recounting an experience. Once, while teaching, he found himself talking to two students who were having a disagreement. Each of them was complaining about the behavior of the other. He met with each of them separately and let them tell their version of what happened. Each of them felt he was in the right. He would have to listen to them together to find out who was telling the truth. But after having thought about this for a while, he decided not to do it. Between Christians there cannot be those who win and those who lose. Putting them together like this might have provoked further discord. The matter at hand was actually not that serious and it wasn't worth it to analyze precisely who was right and who was wrong. It was more important to make them aware of the need to accept one another and through this lead them to mutual pardon. "This was because," he concluded, "on a spiritual level the higher truth is always that which comes from the one Father which makes us all brothers: Love."

Silence. The enchantment of that beautiful moment filled my being. Then, suddenly, a voice called me by name: "And you Matthew, what do you think? Do you agree?"

I remained a little puzzled. Of course I agreed. Taken by surprise I began to offer what was coming to my mind in that moment:

"Certainly, the truth is a mystery that we could go on penetrating forever. . . It is always beyond our reach. Psalm 85 says that up there 'Kindness and truth shall meet; justice and peace shall kiss.' "

I stopped there because I couldn't think of anything else to say. Then a little story I had once read came to mind. Perhaps, even though banal, it had something to do with what we were talking about. I gathered up my courage and began.

"Yes, it is always beyond our reach, but sometimes the question of truth is raised even in the minutiae of every day life."

Once there was a lawyer who, just on principle, would not accept the defence of a client unless he had first tried to be reconciled with his or her adversary first. This system brought him more friends than clients but he was happy with that.

One day, two rivals came to his house. His twelve-year-old son opened the door and then remained in the room to listen.

The lawyer listened to the first man and when he had finished he said, "You're right." The other jumped out of his chair and exclaimed, "But now you have to listen to me." "Certainly, go ahead," said the lawyer. The second man gave his version of the event and at the end, after a moment of reflection, the lawyer concluded, "You're right."

"But father," interrupted the lad, "they can't both be right!"

"You're right, too," said the lawyer.

Laughter broke out among all. With that I thought I had finished, but then as silence fell again I realized that they were waiting for me to offer some kind of a conclusion. "It's true," I observed, "it is hard to know what the truth is. Think of Pilate. He was uncertain as to whether or not he should condemn Jesus who, there before him had affirmed, 'The reason why I came into the world is to testify to the truth.' So Pilate asked him, 'Truth! What does that mean?' But he left before receiving the answer (cf. Jn 18:37-38)."

"The truth," I concluded, "in all its cosmic dimension, was there in that Man. If Pilate couldn't see it when the Truth made flesh was standing there in front of him, no one would have ever been able to explain it to him."

The director now confirmed that the law in force in Loppiano was the law of Love. Its aim was to reach that unity which Jesus had prayed for to the Father. He also added that people often make mistakes, but these mistakes are not sins. People who throughout their political life remained adversaries in the name of a presumed truth, can rediscover both in heaven.

"There are," he concluded, "in personal relationships, moments and particular situations when the desire to seek the truth at any cost can lead to misunderstandings and differences with the truth. Saint Paul himself confirmed it when he said that Love believes all things. Therefore it is possible to support even two people holding opposing views providing that they are in good faith and no one suffers a loss."

By now it was late. We all got up to go home. I said goodbye to those closest to me because the next day I would be leaving for Rome.

When I went to talk to the person responsible for the little city I could not but express my joy and my thanks for what I had seen and heard there. He looked at me squarely: "Why don't you come and live with us?"

I looked at him surprised. I wasn't expecting such an invitation. "Are you serious? Do you think that at my age I could still do something here?"

"Of course! Here more than any other place the presence of an older person would be a precious asset. Every year hundreds of young people come here. They are long on enthusiasm but short on experience. No one, at least today, is capable of offering them the experience of life which has firm roots and yet which is still full of enthusiasm such as yours."

I was moved by this offer and a little uncertain. I muttered a few words, and I departed saying, "Thank you, thank you. I'll think about it."

Returning Home

Intimacy

Vacation was over. We all returned home, that is, to our focolare center in Rome. I sensed a profound peace, perhaps more than my young companions did.

Yes, the mountains, the valleys and the snow-covered peaks are beautiful, but it is also beautiful to rest in the silence of your room where everything that surrounds you—furniture, books and other objects—recalls the fullness of a life that has already been lived, prelude to that which is yet to come. Jesus said: "When you pray, go to your room and, closing the door, pray to your Father in secret" (Mt 6:6).

Intimacy is therefore a solitude which speaks within you and draws you back to yourself, to your true being, with all the spiritual wealth that you have acquired and with the desire for that which you have yet to attain.

Here everything speaks of life, even the awareness of your limitations. Or better, here more than ever you feel the need to turn to the only one who can help you. I do not know any particular prayers to say in these moments of recollection. Rather, in the depths of my heart, I repeat the simple words of the prayers I say every morning: "I adore you my God, I love you with all my heart, with all my soul, with all my mind. I thank you for having created me, for making me a Christian, a Focolarino, and for having called me into your service—full time."

Then comes mealtime and there, around the table, we gather in the joy of a family of people who love one another, so there is laughter and lighthearted conversation.

Then, during moments of meditation and prayer, one is drawn

again into that intimacy with God dwelling within us. Yes, we have an intimate, inner life and an external life, but one is the cause of the growth of the other. Think of a tree. The foliage which lives on the outer part of the tree also causes the development of the root system, and this, in turn, impels the foliage to bloom and bear fruit.

It is the same for us: the more we go out of ourselves to give to others, the more the presence of pure love, Jesus, grows within us. And the more He lives within us the more we tend to give of ourselves to others.

A nice, quiet, little place

This attitude of going out to others may lead to good, earthly friendships, but someone might misunderstand what our life really is.

Today, for example, an old friend and colleague of mine came to visit. He is now a widower and lives alone. Someone—I don't know who—told him about my new "lifestyle," and he thought that my abode could be that nice, quiet, little place he is looking for in which to live out his final days. We sat down together and he asked me if there would be room for him, too, in this house. Of course he would be more than willing to pay his share.

I could have pointed out that space in this house was at a premium so his search for tranquility among us would have been in vain. It's not for nothing, after all, that we are part of a "movement." It seemed more honest, however, to openly explain just what the situation was:

"My dear friend," I began, "I'm not here because one fine day I decided to live in peace with a group of friends. Rather, my being here is the result of my response to a calling that goes back some thirty years. The one who called me, I must tell you, was Him, Christ crucified and risen. Since that time, at least with my heart, I have left everything and followed him. Yes, I have found peace, but it is His peace which is something quite different, if you will allow me to say it, from the peace that you are seeking. The journey I am on, together with my companions, is undertaken in the desire to follow, as much as possible, in Jesus' footsteps, even when he carried the cross, ascended to Calvary, and cried out his abandonment. . ."

My friend listened and showed signs of understanding; he remarked, however, that it didn't seem necessary to cross the borders into the realm of the religious and talk about the cross and Calvary to someone who is merely seeking a refuge wherein to live out his old age.

I couldn't say that he's wrong. But I have to tell him, that in this case, he must look in another direction: "There are hundreds of rest homes where one can conclude one's life in peace and tranquility, maintaining one's habits, remembrances and possessions. To live in the focolare center, instead, means immediate death, leaving one's possessions and forgetting the past in order to start a new life, both active and contemplative, lived in mutual charity. "This," I concluded, "costs a lot, but it gives meaning even to a person on in their years but still young in spirit."

My friend went away sad. But I will not abandon him. I am fully aware of his moral uprightness and I know that his "non-believing" attitude stems more from a reaction to the "lukewarm" Christians he has met.

Besides everything else he is a great admirer and active supporter of the works of Mother Teresa of Calcutta. In fact once, while visiting a boarding school located near my friend's house and operated by her sisters, she stopped by to visit him and thank him for his help.

How I wish my friend could understand that God alone is the driving force behind Mother Teresa's heroic works. She herself said it at the Eucharistic Congress in Pescara, Italy, a few years ago. I, too, was present at that event and great was my surprise at hearing her affirm at the conclusion of her brief talk: "We are not social workers! We are contemplatives!"

Imaginary atheists

This episode led me to observe that many who call themselves atheists in reality are not. The theologian Karl Rahner stated it this way: "Now the Council teaches that even those who call themselves atheists, are connected to the paschal mystery of Christ in the measure in which they follow the dictates of their own conscience which is connected to divine revelation in a way that only God knows."

Another theologian, Deissler, observed: "What is closest to the heart of the God of revelation is the human person, not a particular order, nor a 'religion' in the sense of 'religious practices.' That is why the critical question which the 'Son of man' will ask us regarding our brothers and sisters is that of the 'final judgment' (Mt 25:31-46)."

This is the passage the theologian is referring to:

"Come, O blessed of my Father . . . for I was hungry and you gave me food, I was thirsty and you gave me drink . . . I was a stranger . . . I was naked . . . I was sick and you visited me."

After all, where there is true and selfless love—and therefore the absence of hatred, selfishness, falsity, pride—there is God! And, vice versa, where there is God, there is Love.

I have cited theological texts, but analogous considerations could be advanced on a biological level. Allow me to present the statement in this regard made by Mario Trabucchi, a professor at the University of Padova:

"Modern science explains that life is not determined by a static, biological patrimony. Rather it is the product of the capacity of the individual to be integrated into his or her environment. The one who will enjoy a longer life and a smoother advancement into old age is the one who lives a life rich in relationships, that is, those who are well integrated because of their education or human talents."

But doesn't "integrated" mean "connected, united"? And isn't unity, in its highest expression, the fruit of Love?

What an example then it would be for young people to see old people "well integrated," that is, abounding in attention toward others, in every moment and in every encounter! This holds true also for couples who reach their golden years together. If it is beautiful to see a young married couple, how much more beautiful it should be to see an elderly couple wherein each spouse lives in thoughtful, loving service of the other!

And these couples, once they are free from family commitments, how wonderful if together they could live a life which, integrated into a faith community, allowed time for work, prayer, the giving of oneself and meditation. Besides everything else, in this case the arrival of widowhood would not be synonymous with overwhelming loneliness.

Holy Week

A heart for a heart

Summer passed, and a cold winter as well. Easter time came round and I was spending a few days with my daughter Chiaretta. In the little church dedicated to St. Stephen, close to her house, the words of the readings for Holy Thursday fell on a small group of faithful who were devoted, yes, but a little distracted. I, too, was making an effort to follow. My mind wandered off to thoughts of the people surrounding Jesus. They appeared rather inadequate for the role that awaited them. The only one who seemed to have clear ideas—poor fellow—was Judas. But, let's be honest, who could have really believed in the resurrection, in the victory of life over death?

As I sometimes do on these occasions, I tried to relive the events the gospel was referring to, reconstructing them in my imagination.

Here we are, the evening of the Last Supper. Before sitting down at the table the disciples are having a dispute about which of them is to be regarded as the greatest. Jesus had said, "Let the leader become as one who serves" (cf. Lk 22:26). But, not really having understood these words, a dispute arose. So Jesus gets up, wraps a towel around his waist, gets a basin of water and, kneeling on the ground washes his disciples' feet. Now have they understood?

Then they all gather around the table. Judas is there, troubled, perhaps still doubtful. Jesus invites him to do quickly what he must do. It seemed to me that if he had remained there, closed off in his own thoughts, tormented by atrocious doubts and therefore spiritually divided from the others, Jesus would not have been able to recollect himself in the prayer of the Last

Supper. He wanted to share with his disciples something of his profound unity with the Father, because, forever and ever, the bread he was about to break would become his flesh and the wine his blood. But how could he reach this point if, among the twelve, even only one doubted. At least in that moment "his own" had to be "all one."

Finally Judas goes out and Jesus offers himself to the Father: "This is my body . . . this is my blood." As a divine pelican, it is as if he were giving his heart as food for his children: his heart, that is to say, all of himself. He wants his own to always and evermore relive the supreme sacrifice of that moment.

The disciples participate in this event and sense that that bread is truly his body and that wine is truly his blood. They have watched Jesus multiply the loaves of bread, they have seen him transfigured on Tabor, they remember his words: "The Son of man will be delivered . . . and crucified, and he will be raised on the third day" (Mt 20:18-19).

They had not understood these words when he first said them, but now, gathered together in the Cenacle, they grasp that this is the supreme hour of truth.

I see myself there, in the Cenacle, filled with the desire to understand, to enter into the mystery of that moment. But what can I say, what can I do?

"A heart for a heart" I whisper passionately within myself in the desire to exchange my heart with that ardent heart of Christ. I hide my face in my hands. Immobile, a sense of infinite warmth penetrates within me, almost as if, by miracle, that "heart for a heart" might actually take place.

The "supper" is over. Jesus heads toward Gethsemane together with Peter, James and John who would pray with him. But they fall asleep! He wakes them up, and they fall asleep again!

Poor, dear Jesus! He senses a tremendous emptiness around him and would almost like to put off that moment of extreme sacrifice: "My Father, if it be possible, let this cup pass from me" (Mt 26:39).

But *his hour* has come, and the torment of that agony grips him while drops of sweat as thick as blood, fall to the earth.

I shook myself out of it and looked around. It was time to receive Holy Communion. Everyone got up and I too made my way to the front. I would like to understand more but I can only repeat to myself: "It is you, Jesus, all suffering, all love, it is you."

Tears

Good Friday: the same small flock of faithful, but more recollected than yesterday. I followed the liturgy, and everything spoke of love and suffering.

Then came the moment to venerate the cross. Everyone got up and filed toward the front of the church. I stayed in my place. Yet another river of thoughts poured into me. My soul wanted to love more but experienced only the intense desire to do so.

I observed the others moving slowly along. They were mostly women, as usual. The small crucifix was being held in an upright position by one of the altar boys. The bottom of the cross touched the ground. Most of the people just leaned slightly forward and kissed the image of Christ on the shoulder, or on the arm, and moved on.

The last person was a man. He stopped, somewhat hesitant, before the cross. Then, as if urged by an inner force which he could not resist, he knelt down, lifted the cross and kissed the feet of Christ.

He returned to his place visibly moved, his eyes welling with tears.

Oh, how I understand him! When I admit that, before certain manifestations of the divine, I too am moved to tears, my friends kindly rib me. And someone went even further. A young intellectual, after reading *Lazarus, Come Out,* said in a tone of deep pity, "I found your book quite interesting . . . but, that chapter when you broke into tears at Mass, that was a disaster!"

He could not possibly understand the drama of the person who, already on in years, realizes that he has been violently yanked out of the mainstream of life. Only then does it dawn on him that the game is up, the lights are out and he cannot count on another card being drawn. Life is coming to a close. Then, to suddenly discover that heaven, the fullness of joy, really exists, that it begins even here and now, and that the door by which to enter is still open, this is something that not only leads you to tears, it upsets all the normal parameters for judging life and events. But those are not tears of pain, they are tears of one who is deeply moved.

Jesus, too, cried. He was proceeding toward Jerusalem amidst cheering crowds. But, "when he drew near and saw the city he wept over it, saying, 'Would that even today you knew the things that make for peace!' " (Lk 19:41).

Almost two thousand years have passed since then, and Jesus still weeps for that city of his.

What a profound mystery! But I dare to think that at the dawn of the third millennium Jerusalem will open its eyes and finally "know" what is needed for her to have peace.

One could write an entire treatise on the many occasions where tears are mentioned in scripture. However, if you ask me, there is one episode which, contrary to appearances, the tears do not stem from suffering. It is when Jesus cries as he approaches the tomb of Lazarus whom, shortly after, he would bring back to life.

Certainly no one, myself included, could ever imagine from what infinite depths those tears came forth. He wept, of course, because "he loved him" as those who were present thought. But I think that he cried above all because he was touched in the depths of his soul by the love of the Father. In fact, before the miracle took place, he lifted his eyes to heaven and said: "Father, I thank you because you have heard me." An extraordinary force had entered him and was now about to come out. In no other place, in describing the miracles in which Jesus brought people back to life, do we find the words used on that occasion: "He was deeply moved in spirit and troubled . . . still deeply moved, he came to the tomb . . . and he cried out with a loud voice, 'Lazarus, come out' " (Jn 11:41, 33, 38, 43).

To give our life for one another

It was Holy Saturday evening and I returned home. Gabriele, the Focolarino responsible for our focolare center, was away at a meeting being held at the headquarters of the movement in Rocca di Papa, outside of Rome. All the persons responsible for the focolare centers in Europe, and some from around the world, are meeting together. Not everyone can be accommodated there, however, so each evening Gabriele comes back to Rome to sleep.

Usually he gets home quite late and we have already gone to bed. But one evening we waited up for him and timidly asked how the meeting was going. He only smiled: "When it's all over I'll tell you everything!"

Thus, you can imagine how surprised all five of us were when, early in the afternoon, he called. "Don't go to bed early tonight. I have to tell you something very important."

All the rest of the day we racked our brains in vain trying to guess what the news might be. Each of us ventured a guess, but no sooner had it been formulated than it was discarded.

Finally Gabriele arrived. We all gathered in the dining room.

"I don't know where to begin," he said, visibly moved. "Something happened today that touched me very deeply and gave me a new light with which to see things."

A long pause followed. He looked around at us and, smiling, began again. "Chiara came to talk to us today and in what she said, as she presented her talk on this year's theme—unity—I at first thought that I had heard the concepts before. Ever since I lived in the focolare center with the task of responsibility for its life and events, I have often spoken about this topic. But now, now I realize that I had never really understood unity, 'that' unity for which Jesus came into the world and climbed to Calvary. Of course, because one must in a certain sense 'die' in order to reach it, and I . . . yes, I realize I made many mistakes . . . and now I want to apologize!"

Surprised, all of us, we leaned even further forward. Another pause and Gabriele began again. "When, in the past, I called you bruskly, when I reproached you, I was not completely dead to my own self, and here I was asking you to die to yourselves. . . I didn't take upon myself your suffering, I didn't make it mine, I didn't consume it in love. . . Of course, embracing the suffering of those moments, a certain unity was reached all the same, but it was like 'making do.' It didn't really 'resolve' the matter. There was always a little shadow left behind. And this happened because I was not like a mother who patiently listens to her child until he has really said everything, loving him always, even when she must correct her child."

Another long pause followed. "Sometimes," he said, "I tried to do that, but how many other times I responded out of impatience rather than out of love. Even a correction—now I understand this quite clearly—must be said in such a way that it does not break unity. And this takes place only when each person is ready to give their life for the other."

With this he finished. We sat in silent wonderment for a long time. My fatherly instinct suggested that I get up and embrace him: Gabriele is forty years my junior. But no, here we are all brothers.

It is really Holy Saturday evening. Still moved by the grace received through this meeting, we head out, all together, for midnight Mass. But the joy of the resurrection has already triumphed in our hearts.

A New Type of Elderly Person

Let us go out . . . "to gaze once more at the stars"

The problem of the elderly has come dramatically to the forefront in recent years. Most of the concern, however, is directed toward different forms of assistance. Little is being done, it seems, to better the quality of their life.

When, during the sixties, I worked for the Treasury Department as the head of the Office of Studies and Organization, I thought of a project which would offer low-rate loans to pensioners who, upon leaving the city, wanted to buy a home in the country. The Minister of the Treasury was in favor of this project but, since it involved an issue which was not considered urgent at the time, he put it aside. And that was the end of it.

Today the number of pensioners continues to increase and that proposal could perhaps be used again. What is more, one must consider the fact that these smaller towns are well-suited for that change in the "quality of life" that we all desire. Moreover, since the cost of living in such places is usually lower than in the city, pensioners would be able to manage on the income they receive. Another benefit to this plan is that traffic congestion in the city would decrease to a certain extent and the housing shortage would be relieved. Construction would pick up in these outlying areas. In short the benefits would be reaped by all.

The fact remains that our modern cities have gone beyond the dimension of the human person. The ones who come to my mind in particular are the weaker, those who, for whatever the reason, are no longer as agile as they would need to be to get on and off buses, or make their way in and out of the subway or even just cross the street.

I am not proposing that we invite all the elderly to move to the country. That would be unrealistic. I must confess, however, that I found a principle of urbanistic rationality in some North American cities—from New York to Chicago, from Vancouver to Seattle. These cities do have a center, a jungle of skyscrapers which, by day, act as the converging point, like the brain for all the thinking power. But then there are wide arteries extending out for miles and miles linking the periphery to the brain and along these arteries are strung a myriad of little houses, each with their own front and back yard.

To tell the truth, the human person is, in a certain sense, made the same way.

In the near future, with the aid of technology, urbanistic solutions of this kind will be favored. But I don't want to venture off now into hypotheses regarding our future.

Let us rather try to live "today" well, to give a good example by being the first to go out, as one poet wrote, to gaze once more at the stars. We will rediscover the purity of the environment and the simplicity of life. To aim at this, I think, would be a step toward accomplishing that kind of post-industrial society about which much is said but little is done.

Poor us

As far as assisting the elderly goes, certainly a lot has been said on the topic. I try to keep up with what is going on.

The other day I read something that quite exasperated me. A distinguished professor of economics was asked by the editorial staff of a respectable daily paper for his view on the specific role of senior citizens in today's society. Among other things he said:

> We must consider the function of senior citizens as consumers. It is well known that consumption determines productive activity. Older people are equipped with a certain buying power, especially as their pension matures.

With regard to this, I proposed at a recent convention that we create a special savings structure and type of insurance favorable to the elderly. This was in view of broadening the buying power of the senior citizens, which we depend on in order to maintain production at a certain level.

Poor us! What particularly struck me in this declaration was not the proposed savings structure which, if it came to be, would be beneficial. Rather it was the underlying motive: "We must consider the function of senior citizens as consumers. . ." Of course. Because the elderly, even if they can't do anything else, eat and consume goods.

We find ourselves lowered to the ranks of certain animals who, the more they eat, the fatter they become and the more useful they are to society.

But the absurdity is this: at the same time as these astonishing "discoveries" are taking place, we shed tears over the millions of children in developing nations who are dying of hunger or illness. The contradiction is appalling and yet few bat an eye.

My discoveries, however, now that my attention is drawn to everything that refers to senior citizens, do not end here.

Here is another type of solution which is a fruit of the initiative of the town council of a small northern city. The two column heading in the paper read:

Are you elderly, with problems?
Talk it over with your dog.

The text which summarizes the substance of this ingenious discovery is the following:

"We would like to offer our citizens, and above all, young students, a point of reflection. In order to avoid misunderstanding and mutual rejection between two very important age groups—children and the elderly—may we suggest that they enter into an exchange of ideas on a topic such as dogs. The antics of this lively animal help pave the way to encounter and dialogue.

44

The following is an excerpt from the journalist's commentary:

How can it be that loneliness and rejection stem from a misunderstanding about dogs, and that things will work out when pensioners and children begin to organize roundtable discussions and dialogue about leashes and the quality of dog food?

If this were really the case we would be just one step away from the solution to all the problems afflicting the elderly. So it's not a matter of sufficient hospital beds nor dignified and welcoming rest homes available to all. . . What's really missing is canine conversation!

I wholeheartedly share the journalist's lashing irony. But what about me? I naively thought it was my task to help the older person gradually rise above the level of material needs and enter the sphere of spiritual life. It seems that's not the case, though. According to certain psychologists, it is better for the elderly to step down a peg to the level of the animals!

Don't think I have it against dogs—poor things! They have even aroused my affection at times, so I can appreciate certain viewpoints. But there is a limit!

In the book *The Elderly and Us* by Pino Quartana, I read of an episode that actually took place and that quite shocked me. I should mention that it is not an isolated case:

After a two-month stay in the hospital the daughter of the elderly patient was called in by the attending physician, Dr. Finzi, from Venice.

"Your father is better now. You can take him home."

"No doctor, I can't."

"Why not?"

"I can't, because now I have a dog. He's gotten bigger in these past two months and he doesn't like to be around older people."

"Well, give the dog away!"

"Oh, I couldn't, I've grown very fond of him!"

Any comment on this would be quite superfluous! But, I repeat, it's not that I have anything against dogs!

The disillusioned social worker

Now my eyes have fallen upon an article from a past issue of a Christian magazine. The heading is "The Elderly and Us." The title is rather startling:

Elderly people today:
unpleasant and selfish

Here are some lines from a letter written by one of the magazine's readers, a social worker.

I would like to talk about those sweet, helpless and needy old people who pluck at our heartstrings. I have seen very few of them.

Believe me, children do not always abandon their elderly parents out of selfishness. That's what I used to think. Now I have worked for many years as a social worker in an old age home and I have seen that the elderly can be disagreeable, resentful toward the world and young people, selfish.

Seventy percent of them are like that. They are not ones to reciprocate; rather they are quite demanding. Old people in the past were better: meek and wise, they cared for their neighbor, maybe their diet then was simpler and more moderate. Instead (people have told me) many old people today never lived a physically and mentally balanced life. They never helped other people or had consideration for those around them.

The editor's comment, after such an assertion was, needless to say, meek. He attempted to justify the elderly, quoting the pope's talk in Munich, Germany, on November 19, 1980:

Old age is marked by a process of withering; the world and its concerns seem foreign, life is heavy, the body a torment. The burden of age renders the body more fragile, sensory perception is no longer as acute, the limbs are no longer agile, one's organs are more vulnerable. . . The elderly person often loses familiarity with the world of his or her own family, with economy and politics and even with the teachings of the Church.

It's all true! But it is also true, as our social worker pointed out, that older persons of our generation are almost never prepared to face old age.

How can we not agree? I, too, have written that these thoughts of mine on the golden years are aimed, above all, at those who have not yet reached that point.

One must be prepared, therefore, in body and spirit. As for the body, there are countless specialists in geriatrics, ready to give advice on diet and exercise. As far as the spirit goes, we gain some insight into the situation as we read the last paragraph of the aforementioned letter. Our disillusioned social worker, in fact, after fully describing the negative side of older people, continued:

I am certain that only a very holy nun could comprehend these people. I cannot make it any more and I am really disgusted, even if at one time I believed I had great love for my neighbor. I have decided now to give up on that group of people and dedicate myself, perhaps, to children or elderly priests. What do you think? Is this morally right or am I just being selfish?

Perhaps at this point our friend is waiting to be absolved of her sins. If I were a priest I could do so. Also because in this last reflection of hers she has grasped, even if indirectly, the heart of the matter. That is, she would be ready for anything, if it meant to take care of people who are loving.

So here we are back where we started. Do we want to help those approaching their golden years? Let us invite them to prepare themselves ahead of time to meet and understand one another. Then, of course, the practices of piety and prayer in common, such as are found in nursing homes run by religious orders, are welcome additions. But if, for the guests, this remains just a formality, that is, if it is not the expression of a corresponding inner life, one wonders what benefit it has.

The bottom line, therefore, is that we should prepare ourselves for the years ahead, as many as the Lord and his goodness may grant us. Let's do it by meeting together; by giving Jesus the central place in our lives, by learning how to walk in his footsteps. Thus, when we reach the age of fragility it will be easier to find someone to understand and help us.

It is Hard to Love

Letter to an eighteen-year-old

Affluence has made us selfish. The more you have the more you want. When you think you are free, you want to be even more free: a lot of confusion stems from this, and a lot of misunderstanding.

It is also true that the rules of the game have changed in today's world. But deep down they are always the same: true love is love which reaches the point of sacrifice of self, of one's time, of one's viewpoint.

It is not really accurate to assume that the "capacity to love" is greater among the young than the not so young. Just a few days ago I received a desperate letter from an eighteen-year-old girl. She is going from crisis to crisis. She can't make it to love anyone: neither her family at home, nor people outside.

I often receive letters like this. They are written by people who have met me through one of my books, or at a conference, and they feel comfortable with me just because of my age. Mine, after all, is not the age of dreams, but that of life experience.

But can I—a grandfather for over twenty years—touch the heart of an eighteen-year-old? I do not know, and yet I must try. The following is my answer to her letter of desperation.

Dear . . . ,

In your last letter you confided that your moments of crisis have returned and that you can't find "a way out." I think, however, that all this is happening because you have not yet found "a way in," the only way that gives meaning to our life. And that is the way of "Love."

Now you will tell me that if a person doesn't feel love

inside then she can't be expected to show it on the outside. But this is true only on a human level. I am talking about a kind of love that reaches the measure of sacrifice. And by this I mean that we demonstrate the "will to love," even if it costs our very life.

Why not take a fresh look at those you live with. If they don't understand you, try to understand them. If they don't smile at you, you be the first to smile at them. Offer your help to someone. Is love missing in your home or at your place of work? Well, put love and there you will find love. It will all come back to you, and at this point you will find the joy which up until now you have been searching for in vain. The one who loves, in fact, enjoys the fullness of life, while the one who does not love is like one of the walking dead.

To reach this goal it may take a revolution: first of all a revolution inside of you, and then around you. But you will not be alone. By now there are millions, all over the world, committed to achieving this goal.

Start right away! Smile at the next person you meet as soon as you finish reading this letter; then smile at the next, and then the next.

Of course, you won't be able to do too much by yourself. Try to keep in close contact with others who have already set out along this way. I know that you know some of them who live right in your town.

My dear young friend, I feel close to you as to one of my own daughters. Take courage! I am sure that you will make it to overcome yourself; and you will finally be happy!

Three months later her answer arrived. It didn't exactly inspire enthusiasm. "Yes," the young lady wrote: "What I long for most is to encounter God within me . . . and tomorrow I have an appointment with the psychologist."

I seem to have made a mistake. Evidently she expected to hear something else. But will the psychologist know how to lead her to God, the one she is seeking?

Ah well! To love and to serve is hard for me, too, even though I long to do so with all my heart. But your heart is not enough. You must also be aware of all the other aspects involved so as to fully grasp the entire matter and really look at it from your neighbor's point of view.

Bertrand Russell, ever bitter but realistic, said that at the bedside of a gravely ill person it is preferable to have a good doctor whose soul may be corrupt than a dear friend of noble spirit but ignorant in medicine.

He may have been right.

Mothers-in-law

To love and to help others to do the same, is, therefore, difficult. And this is true also because each one of us is a unique being. More often than not we err by defect and this happens when we do not bring things to a conclusion. Sometimes, however, we err by excess, such as when we do more than is needed.

That was the case of the elderly lady who came to visit me today because she needed to share her troubles. She has four sons, all married, and is grandmother to many grandchildren. Now she is a widow, living alone, but still filled with energy. And so she busies herself with everything and everyone.

A good Christian no doubt, she certainly means well. "But often," she told me, "I'm rejected by my children. I get the impression that it bothers them to see me coming . . . but I never ask them for anything. I listen to their problems, but what do I get for it? Indifference, even rudeness, at times . . . what should I do?"

I certainly understood. Her problem is the solitude that many, even though well meaning, find themselves suddenly immersed in. The family was everything for them. They never really bothered about the neighbor next door or about their fellow parishioners.

I've seen, too, that this problem is particularly common among mothers-in-law, like the one that had sat in front of me. My impulse was to tell her that love must be "intelligent," and by that I mean, capable of "reading" the other person. One cannot just interfere any time or any place. And yet . . . I let her go on talking so that she could let go of her whole burden. I wanted to take upon myself all the anguish burdening her spirit.

In the end, the truth came out, and she herself discovered it after she had been freed from all her bitterness. "Perhaps . . . yes, I suppose I have held on too tightly to my sons . . . I interfere too much in their lives. I impose my ideas on them and they probably feel I'm trying to control them. But I'm all alone, all alone. . . At dinner time I don't even bother to set the table any more . . . I just munch on something and walk about the kitchen."

A dinner guest

I observed her in silence; then with great cordiality I began. "Are you so sure that you're alone? I think you know Jesus, don't you?"

She nodded but remained silent.

"Then why do you feel alone?" I asked. "If you want, He is with you always, even at meal time."

She questioned me with her eyes. I went on. "Try setting the table as if you were expecting a guest. Then sit down and, as you begin to say grace, remember Him and those words he said: 'Behold I stand at the door and knock; if anyone hears my voice and opens the door, I will come in to him and eat with him, and he with me' (Rev 3:20)."

My friend smiled, her eyes brightened and she exclaimed, "Thank you, thank you so much. Now I know! I won't be alone anymore. He will always be there, across from me."

She was truly moved. We exchanged a few more words, but

as she got up to leave, she repeated once again, "Thank you, thank you so much."

A little less than a month later a letter arrived from her. She was enthusiastic. Apparently as soon as she got home it was supper time and she set the table carefully. Her thoughts turned to Jesus. She wrote:

I was almost tempted to put a napkin at the place across from me, but then I knew it wasn't necessary. I felt his presence all the same.

I've continued to follow your advice and my life has really changed. I don't drop in on my children and grandchildren every day. Now they're coming to visit me, sometimes they even bring a little gift. They used to see me so sad all the time, and now they're amazed to see me always smiling. But I know the reason behind this joy. It comes from that Friend you brought me to know in a much more intimate way.

I would never have imagined that the advice I gave would have brought such success. The idea had just come to me on the spot. I decided to try it again on another dear friend who came to visit. She too was a widow, living alone, visiting her son who lived in my focolare center in Loppiano. She, too, found these words to be quite a revelation. Here is what she later wrote to me:

The words of Jesus that you shared with me are truly marvelous. I didn't really know them before. What a discovery for me, and what a change they have brought about! I understand that in the little things of life it's important to remember that we are all children of God and that he loves us immensely.

Now, when meal time comes, I set the table just as you suggested and I turn off the television . . . I sit down with Him and I share with Him all that is in my heart, including all about your Focolare. I sense that He is listening, I sense His patience. He's truly a wonderful dinner partner. . .

Here, besides the understandable enthusiasm over the discovery of a Jesus who comes to be with us, I was struck by another comment: "I set the table just as you suggested and I turn off the television. . ."

Now that's wisdom!

Learning how to die. . .

Up until now we have spoken of the need to "learn how to love." But that's not enough. Cicero once affirmed: "We need to learn how to die."

Death is often considered a topic that one shouldn't even think about. But there are also those who, once they have reached a certain age, serenely begin to consider it. Most, however, suffer anguish at the thought, and do nothing to start the process of letting go of their home, their possessions, business and interests, because these things, experts say, help people to live. But, say I, they don't help you to die!

Culture centers and universities are reaching out, more and more, to senior citizens, encouraging them to take an interest in some aspect of life such as medicine, literature, art, history, economics, foreign languages, music, archeology.

It's hard to imagine, however, that a person dying with cancer of the liver who is happy just because he or she has mastered Chinese or has become an expert in Etruscan art.

This might be alright for some people, but it surely cannot satisfy those who, in the course of their life, have encountered a "greater light." Having come from eternity and being directed towards eternity, we should be able to offer our last smile as a gift to the person next to us. Then dying would simply mean, "So long, for now."

However, like it or not, even an elderly non-believer must consider the other side of the coin—the side facing the final horizon. His or her greatest concern then will not be that of getting back into the flow of life, but rather of gradually retreating from the stage of this world so as to better search for a new way of aging. By this I mean not shutting oneself off but attempting to overcome one's selfishness, to go out to all, smiling and contemplating the mysteries of life—birth and death—in which we are all immersed.

Indeed this mystery will always remain shrouded by one last veil, but it will reveal something of itself to the one who contemplates it, with love, in God. At that point sickness and old age will no longer be seen as a decline, but rather as a purification. And it will be possible to say of these people: "Old age did not bring about decline, rather consecration." These words of the liturgy which refer to Our Lady's maternity could then be applied to them.

Every once in a while someone of the community will leave for heaven, but the funeral will resemble more a celebration. All will be present: young and old, men and women. Perhaps their songs will be laced with tears but in the end someone will say: "How beautiful it is to die like this!" Of those who attended my wife Teresa's funeral many displayed just such wonder through expressions like that.

We must be aware that this is truly a great revolution. St. Paul was right in asserting: "O death, where is your victory? O death, where is your sting?" (1 Cor 15:55).

But Christendom has not fully awakened yet. In vain Christ calls out: "Lazarus, come out!"

That invitation. . .

Today was a hard day for me. I returned home exhausted, and so late that my friends were quite alarmed.

Three months ago I had asked my eye doctor for an appointment and today was the day. Knowing that the transport workers were calling wildcat strikes I left in plenty of time. I had to get across the city and it meant transferring three times.

The bus stop was crowded. The few buses that passed by were filled to overflowing. Only the people at the very front made it to get on and I couldn't bring myself to push and shove my way in.

Finally, I made it to get on but I will spare you the description of the scene. When my transfer stop was approaching I began elbowing my way to the door and squeezed out. Here another crowd awaited. And it would be more difficult for me now because we were right downtown. Only one of the many different buses that passed by here would take me to my destination. But because of my eyesight I couldn't make out the number of the bus until it was very close. The others, instead, could see it from afar and ran ahead of me to get in line. So there I remained on the sidewalk.

The minutes ticked by and I became more and more apprehensive. I should be at the doctor's office by now. If I miss this appointment it will be months before I get another one. I was losing my peace. Suddenly I spotted a taxi. I ran toward it but someone else got there first. After a while another came along, and then another, but, being full, they didn't even stop.

I then decided on a more radical approach. No matter what bus stopped I decided I would get on it. They all followed the same route at least for the first few blocks. If it weren't mine, I would get off at the next stop.

I climbed aboard the first bus that came. Unfortunately it wasn't my bus so with shouts of "Excuse me, excuse me" I made my way to the exit. I climbed aboard the next one. At last! My bus! I had made it. Off we headed toward the outskirts of the city. I knew I would only have to wait a little for the third bus.

All went well. "Oh, how beautiful the city is, how big the city is." Someone sang these words many years ago. Sure, it was beautiful, but not for me. I didn't want to grow old in this hell. I wanted to get out as fast as I could.

With that a light suddenly went on and an image came to mind—a sun-bathed hill, a friendly voice whispering: "Why don't you come and live with us?"

That was the invitation extended to me last July by my friends in Loppiano—that threshold to heaven where, who knows why, everyone smiles.

Oh, how I would love to go back there. Perhaps that was the ideal place—in every sense of the word—for those like me who have reached their golden years but who still want to live. "But," I asked myself, "will I make it to follow through with the commitment that this new life implies?"

"Yes," I told myself, "I am ready!" I reflected again: Loppiano is not a resort, there are no rest homes for senior citizens. What would I do there?

I could try, though. I could thank God for that Jesus who shines forth from the eyes and smiles of the young people at Loppiano and at the same time I could be a living witness of the love of God which changed my whole life, renewing it from the bottom up.

Yes, I could try! Why waste any more time tossing the idea back and forth?

To leave everything

I returned to the focolare and talked about it with my friends. They all agreed. Next I spoke with the Focolarino responsible for our zone. He, too, basically agreed that I should accept the invitation, but our conversation concluded with what I thought was a rather vague "Good, we'll discuss it again."

A little disappointed I headed for the door to leave. But then I turned around and began again: "To tell you the truth, if it is possible for me to go to Loppiano, I would like to go right away. You know how old I am: I'm in good health and I still have a little energy. But if I wait too long what will I bring to Loppiano? A bag of worn out bones? I have to say it's now or never!"

The case was clear and the answer likewise: "Fine then, we'll make it now!" Arrangements were made and a date was set. I would arrive in Loppiano on December 8, four days from then.

The year was 1981. That day I turned seventy-seven, and I was off, rather unwittingly, on a new adventure.

But the inner upheaval was just beginning. Once again I would have to leave everything, even the little I had been left with after leaving the beautiful house on Padova Avenue and moving into the focolare center downtown. It had been hard at first because the house itself was darker, the area noisier. But then I had gotten used to it and I had even grown to like it. Now everything was being cut away . . . even the weekly visits to my daughter's house . . . even Rome, this city where I had lived, loved and suffered for fifty years.

But no, no regrets! I threw my heart past the obstacle and now, like the horsemen on show, I had to make the leap to retrieve it.

We would leave in the afternoon, so around noon I headed out to make a few purchases. I looked around me and crossed the bridge over the Tiber. Sea gulls were circling close by. How beautiful they were. But no, I had to leave them, I didn't want to look at them anymore—neither them nor anything else. Rome, I don't want to look at you anymore!

These pain-filled words reminded me of other words I had heard: "I pass through Rome and I don't want to look at it." They were the words of Chiara Lubich!

This heart-rending sigh sprang to her lips when she moved to Rome from her native Trent. She had always considered it to be the city of martyrs and saints, but now. . .

I took in hand the collection of the first issues of Città Nuova Magazine.* They were mimeographed pages.

In the October 15 issue I found the piece I was looking for:

If I look around Rome as it is now, I feel our Ideal is far off, as far off as are the days when the great saints and martyrs illuminated even the walls of this city.

Now the world and its vanities reign in its streets and squares. I would have to say our Ideal is a utopia if it weren't

---

* The Italian version of Living City Magazine

for Him. He too looked upon the crowds and loved them. He had come to earth to draw the family together: to make all one. And instead, in spite of His words of fire that dissolved the trifling vanities, people, most of the people, did not want to understand Him and remained with their eyes closed.

He looked at the world as I do, but He did not doubt. By night he prayed to the heavens above and the heaven within Him, whereas outside, the nothingness that passes, lingered in the streets. I too want to do as He did, to remain constantly in the Eternal, to believe in the victory of light over darkness.

I pass through Rome and I don't want to look at it. . .

But the writing goes on. Chiara opens her eyes and discovers, in the frivolity, in the materialism and in the vanities of the world around her the very countenance of Jesus crucified and forsaken: a world, therefore, that more than any other needs to be loved so as to be saved.

Here I am Lord!

But now, just as I'm about to leave Rome, the city I don't want to see anymore, what's come over me? Waves of nostalgia?

All it took was a phone call from a very dear friend—which reached me just as I was at the door, suitcase in hand—for me to realize that besides the Rome made of stone and monuments, noble and sacred but without a soul, besides the anonymous crowds flowing in and around it, and besides the advertising spread all around it, there is another Rome. It is a Rome made up of persons with ardent and pure hearts, persons bound to me because of the many years during which we journeyed, suffered and rejoiced together.

"Yes," I said, "I'm leaving. Goodbye."

I paused for a moment, my hand still on the receiver. I surprised even myself by letting out a long, sorrowful sigh. Then my hand moved to pick up the suitcase which somehow seemed even heavier now. I couldn't postpone it any more. It was time to leave. I had to put my feelings aside.

Out of the tumult of contrasting emotions came a thought: "He who places his hand on the plow and then looks back is not fit for the kingdom of God" (cf. Lk 9:62). Let's go. Someone is already outside honking the horn to say he's ready.

"I'm coming, I'm coming!"

Lord, be patient. First you give us a heart of flesh and then . . . you yourself said that "the spirit is willing but the flesh is weak." Well then? At least allow me to sigh.

Jesus does not get offended in these cases. He is a friend. You can tell him everything. It is pleasant to depart like this. It is like a peaceful death.

The car was ready downstairs. It was already dark. And it became even darker as we left the lights of the city behind. They had offered some assurance in spite of everything.

It was pouring rain. For some reason, the darkness of the night, the rain beating down, the car speeding along defiantly, it all made me feel more fearful. I was trembling inside. Help me, my God!

Three hours later we left the highway and headed toward Incisa Valdarno. We crossed over the Arno River, turned right, then left, and then roared up a steep hill.

It was raining harder than ever, and the wind rose up against us. Would we make it to the top?

But wait, could it be a coincidence? On a December day like this one, in 1943, a person chosen by God made her way up a hill, struggling against a storm to make it to her place before an altar and pronounce her yes to God.* She too had the impression that someone, furious, was trying to stop her. But her yes was said and thousands more came afterwards, including mine. A yes that I now repeated and confirmed with all the strength of my will.

---

* The author is referring to Chiara Lubich's consecration to God which took place on December 7, 1943.

We made it. The car drew to a stop. But where? Everything was dark. I got out and looked around.

There was a house and, not far away, a row of black cypresses. At the sound of the horn a few young men came to the door: hello, hello! They greeted me as if they had known me all their lives. My friends who had accompanied me said goodbye and left. I went into the house: that is, the focolare of my new friends.

Their smiling faces and the warmth of the kitchen where a large table was set and ready reassured me and brought me in turn to smile and offer a word or two. All of them knew at least something about me. But I knew nothing about them so one by one they introduced themselves. They were eight altogether: two Brazilians, one Filipino, three Italians, one Swiss and one Lebanese.

Pierino

Pierino, the gardener, was the person responsible for this focolare. He was some forty years my junior but he and I both knew that before God, age makes no difference. We are all just barely born and we go around stammering the letters of the alphabet that make up the word "Love" in order to be able to live it in its entire universal dimension.

It was supper time and the young men took their places around the table. I looked at them, and they looked at me. No one moved.

Of course, I thought, they're waiting for me to say grace.

The solemnity of the moment struck me deeply—the grace of being able to sit down with these young people. Besides the act of thanksgiving to God for what he gives us, it was for me almost a call to brotherly *agape*. There was love burning in our hearts.

I slowly pronounced the words of the Hail Mary. I had the clear sensation that the fullness of something sacred was entering our hearts.

The dinner conversation was simple and cordial. At one point I would have liked a bit of wine but I was careful not to ask for it. On the table there was only a pitcher of water. Pierino, however, read my thoughts. "Maybe you would like a little wine . . . we don't have any but from now on, if you prefer, we can buy some."

"Oh, that's alright," I responded rather unenthusiastically. Then I saw that there was no fruit on the table but again I said nothing. Pierino noticed this too. "We have no fruit this evening because we shared what we had with some young people who came to visit this afternoon."

Our conversation continued a little further. Then they showed me around the house. It was an old farm house that had been abandoned by its landowners years ago and was now renovated by us.

The room they showed to me was quite large and there were two beds. Pierino, however, assured me that I would have the room to myself. We went ahead and came to another big room which had four beds, all assigned. I began to feel somewhat ill at ease. How could I keep an unoccupied bed in my room while they slept four in another room? I would have to see what to do.

We got ready to say the evening prayers together. The day's happenings faded into the past. Gathered around in a circle we looked at one another. We were so different one from the other. And yet we felt so united, our souls were at peace. Our prayer rose up humbly as if from one heart: "Our Father, who art in heaven. . ."

I retired to my room. To get to the bathroom, however, I had to go down a long corridor. I went, but on my way back I ended up in the dining room. What did I see there? Pierino curled up on a mattress on the floor.

I excused myself, but then I stopped for a moment and said, "But what's this. There's an empty bed in my room and you're here sleeping on the floor."

"It's just for now," he replied. "Then we'll organize everything. It's better like this for now."

Finally I too stretched out in bed. The rain and the wind beat against the little window that looked out over the fields. A vague sense of fear overcame me: the winter will be long and hard. Where was that Tabor? Where were those soft rolling hills with that beautiful green field where I met last summer with the hundred or so young people who listened to someone speaking with such a sense of fascination that you couldn't help but think of Jesus? I, too had been there, behind everyone else, listening, fascinated.

Now it seemed to have disappeared. But the reality, the plan of God for me could not have changed. I felt sure of that: I was here to bear witness, whether summer or winter, through my silence or with my words. In terms of elderly people I am the only one, at least for now, but I am not isolated. I am not young but I have learned how to live in the midst of young people. I, too, like everyone else, will have a task: to meditate, to contemplate, to know and bring to others the love Jesus brought on earth; and then to lose myself in him when my hour comes.

The Civilization of Love

A new sense of solidarity

I have been a citizen of Loppiano for two years now and I still can't help trying to come up with a reason as to why the Lord granted me the grace of living up here.

What particularly surprises me about Loppiano is the steady increase in the number of visitors. Yesterday, Sunday, 1,200 people came for the day. What is it that attracts them to this place?

One answer, which I didn't expect, was proposed by a young man from Rimini, Italy, who came for the day. When he was asked his impression of Loppiano he replied: "Here the Ideal at the basis of your life has become your very civilization."

This was quite a revelation for me. I was struck by the depth of those few words. For our young people the Ideal, as we speak of it, is God. For it to become our "civilization" means having brought about, through Love, that unity for which Jesus prayed before dying: "Father, that all may be one . . . that they may become perfectly one" (Jn 17:22-23). In concrete terms it means injecting into the circuit of social life a new and higher meaning of solidarity.

Before Pope Paul VI coined the term expressing that wonderful image—"the civilization of Love"—we aimed at a future in which humanity would reach a higher level of understanding and mutual tolerance to the point of forming the "United States of the World." Finally we would have understood that "it's not worth it" for one person to devour another.

But the absence of war is not yet peace. A state of mutual tolerance is not yet the kind of civilization we long for. One can talk about peace even while remaining safely at home.

At an international meeting of the New Humanity Movement of the Focolare on March 23, 1983 Chiara Lubich stated:

We know that as human beings we carry within ourselves, like a wound that will not heal, a longing for the supernatural: the divine torments us, the infinite haunts us, and the eternal attracts us.

We know that even if we succeed in renewing all of humanity, in actually building a new world, our hearts will still not have attained all that we yearn for.

Why? Because we have been made for a life that never ends. In building the earthly city we can begin right now to construct something that will not pass away, because we can contribute to the "new heavens," and the "new earth" that await us.

In fact, in redeeming the universe, Christ redeemed human activities as well. Indeed, he has redeemed the works of people as well. The universe will not be annihilated but transformed. There will be no rupture between this world and the next but continuity.

But this will only come about under one condition: our works will remain if they have been carried out in this world according to the commandment of love.

I let myself become completely absorbed by this, reading the last words of the text over and over again. I barely registered the knock on the door of my room. "Come in, come in," I called out without getting up.

A grey-haired man entered. At first I didn't recognize him. Then I exclaimed: "Well, look who's here! Aristides! Is it really you?" He smiled and nodded.

I wanted to be happy

He is an old colleague-friend of mine who had tried to look me up at the focolare center in Rome. Not finding me, he continued his journey to Loppiano, wanting to still nourish our friendship. Apparently, in spite of everything, he finds in my life and my surroundings something that attracts him.

We greeted each other warmly as always. "I apologize for disturbing you," he said. "What were you reading?"

I hesitated for a moment and then I began to briefly explain the text before me, reading aloud the last lines: "our works will remain if they have been carried out according to the commandment of love."

My friend sat in silence, then he exclaimed: "Pardon me, but this is mere poetry. Love . . . evangelical love . . . it's all well and good, but you can't live on it!"

"Perhaps it is poetry," I replied. "But think about it for a moment. Isn't poetry the transfiguration of a reality we are all aiming at? Tell me the truth, why did you come all the way to Loppiano? Wasn't it because of that undefinable something that attracts you?"

"Yes, it's true. I've said it before. But I live in Rome. You have to be tough if you want to survive in that chaos. You have to defend yourself from everyone and everything."

"I understand my dear friend. I lived there too for fifty years. Yes, before knowing Christ I had to be tough, as you say, to survive, but then I discovered that I had to be even tougher if I wanted to 'live,' that is, if I wanted to attain the 'fullness of soul' I desired. Do you know what I mean? I wanted to be happy."

My friend looked at me in amazement. I continued. "But to reach that I had to first of all overcome the selfishness that lay smoldering within me. Then I had to step out of myself and go towards others, friends and enemies alike, without counting the cost, and so on, and so on . . . you know my story."

"I know, I know," my friend added softly, "but there is also truth to the proverb that says that if you act like a lamb, you'll be eaten by a wolf."

"Yes, yes . . . but you see there are lambs, and lambs . . . There are those lambs that graze peacefully under the watchful eye of the shepherd, ready to flee when the wolf approaches. And there are those who become both lamb and shepherd at the same time. And when his moment comes he allows himself to be eaten. He sacrifices himself, but the rest of the flock is saved: humanity, both now and in the future. Do you follow me? This lamb, I'm sure you've understood, is Jesus."

My friend lowered his head, confused. He had nothing else to say. Perhaps it was wrong of me to bring him so suddenly to face the reality of the crucified Lamb.

And yet, no. He lifted his head, smiled and apologized.

The hundredfold

To ease our mutual sense of embarrassment I suggested that we go out for a walk and stop for a cup of coffee. He willingly agreed. As we walked we commented on spring's late arrival and soon I was able to approach the previous topic once again.

"You see," I began, "in Jesus there certainly are also those characteristics of goodness and kindness that we accentuate when we speak about him to children, and often to adults for that matter. But there is a severe side to him as well. Remember when he chased the moneychangers out of the temple and knocked over their tables (cf. Mk 11:15)? Think of the parable of the wise and foolish virgins, and the one about the talents that were distributed in an unequal manner. It's in the gospel of Matthew, chapter twenty-five.

"Obviously these parables contain a meaning which transcends a strictly literal interpretation. But even if you took them at face value alone and applied them to everyday circumstances they do contain an important lesson. Christ is the greatest realist of human history."

My friend looked at me somewhat perplexed as if to say, "Well then?"

I continued. "In the first case Jesus, the bridegroom, promptly leaves outside the door the foolish virgins who, because of their lack of foresight, let their lamps go out. In the second case we hear about a man who received just one talent and hid it underground so that no one would steal it. Jesus scolds him because he didn't even deposit it in a bank which at least would have given interest, and he punishes the man by taking away the one talent he had."

At this point my friend's face brightened and he laughed heartily. "Look at that," he exclaimed, "I never noticed before that the gospel gives credibility to banks and their function!"

"Of course," I said. "And St. Paul explains it very well when he said that 'all are yours; and you are Christ's; and Christ is God's (1 Cor 3:22-23).' Jesus actually puts us in charge of the world and lets us free to undertake any activity. What counts is that these activities are carried out honestly and in consideration of the common good.

"If we want to remain on this level we should remember that the gospel also talks about another kind of bank: a bank in which 'good actions' are deposited. This bank gives extremely good interest."

"Really? How much?"

"Guess. . ."

"Twenty, thirty percent?"

"Oh much, much more my dear friend: one hundred percent!

"But it can't be! I know something of the gospel. I go to church every Sunday . . . but I've never heard them talk about this 'bank' as you call it."

"Well take a careful look at chapter ten of Matthew's gospel. There you will find it written that the one who knows how to become poor of everything and place himself at his neighbor's service and announce the good news (that is, perform good works), Jesus promises to give this person the hundredfold."

"Oh, now I understand! It's Paradise."

I stopped, amazed. That's exactly what it is. But I hadn't planned on reaching that conclusion so quickly. I started again.

"Yes, that's what it is, but the wonderful part of it is that you can receive the hundredfold right here and now!"

"That's incredible. It can't be . . . it's just too beautiful."

"But wait . . . it is also written there that all these things will be 'accompanied by persecutions.' "

My friend fell silent. He studied my face and timidly ventured a question. "Is that true? Is that how it was for you?"

"I never suffered actual persecution . . . but tribulations, yes, many of them, especially at the beginning. However, you have to take into account that the hundredfold that arrives is in relation to the value of what was left behind. I began when I was fifty years old and I had little to leave. But all the same I will receive the hundredfold for the little I left because, after all, it was my everything."

Experiences

It's not a shrine...

Today, like every Sunday, buses pull into Loppiano from all over Italy and other European countries. A young man approached me and with quite a thoughtful air about him asked, "Is this the church?"

"No," I replied, "this isn't a church. It's a building that was at first constructed as a printing plant. But that project wasn't continued and the building was remodelled as a meeting place."

"Oh, I see . . . I came here at the invitation of my pastor. They had told me that a lot of people come here on Sundays and I was expecting to find a shrine, or an abbey like in Pompeii and Assisi."

"We don't have anything like that here in Loppiano. But Mass will be celebrated at noon."

I read the disappointment on the young man's face. He looked around before fixing his gaze on the big building that was about to swallow him up. With a note of sadness he continued, "So this is where the conferences are held."

"Well, they're not exactly conferences, more like meetings. You'll see, it's very interesting. There are also young people who sing."

That young man was looking for a shrine. Perhaps I should have told him that, in a certain sense, this is a shrine. A little different from others, but a shrine. It is commonly thought that a shrine is an ancient place, rich in memories and works of art, famous for its miracles. New interest has been displayed in such places recently. In fact, Pope John Paul II, addressing a group of seminary rectors in January 1981, said that a shrine "is a place where the heart of God's people beats in a particular way . . .

and responds to the need to find a place where the divine has revealed itself."

Many come to Loppiano; can it be said that the hearts of those who come "beat in a particular way"? I hope so.

The meetings begin with an explosion of songs sung by members of the two musical groups performing alternately. They are songs of joy based on the words of the gospel. Then, one by one, the individual members of the group introduce themselves and a murmur rises from the audience as it learns how many nations these young people come from. Besides the Europeans, there are Filipinos, Africans, Chinese, Koreans, Americans. The songs are messages transmitted through words and music, but above all through the light that shines through the eyes of these young people and enters the hearts of those who watch and listen. This is already a form of dialogue because everyone, those who sing and those who listen, are immersed in a mysterious presence of love: a wave that departs, arrives and returns.

After the songs, personal experiences are shared which tell of the new life that is being lived after the encounter with God. Young people and adults, engaged and married couples offer their stories. Their aim is to give praise to God. They imitate Mary who, as humble as she was, proclaimed: "From now on all generations will call me blessed; for He who is mighty has done great things for me"(Lk 1:48-49).

A heart that still wants to beat

I am collecting the texts of the most powerful experiences shared on living the gospel. Here is one that was given today by Tony Daga, one of the young people (he is just over twenty) living here in Loppiano. I find it interesting particularly because it shows in how many different ways the word Love can be concretely lived. It is after all a word which is interpreted in many different ways by those who do not understand its pure and divine beauty.

71

The young man went up on stage and looked around as if he had a problem he needed to solve. He hesitated and then began:

I would like to tell you the story of my conversion, that is, the story of how I made it to radically change my life from the moment I understood that "the one who loves lives, not the one who expects to be loved." But I think it will be more interesting if I tell you how I tried to apply this principle in my particular environment.

The young man stopped and looked around, altering the tone of his voice as someone does when they want to share something very personal.

Actually I was told to be brief, but I would have many small episodes to recount, so I will concentrate on just a few, simple flash experiences.

When I was in my last year of college, concluding my studies in foreign languages, I needed to find a way to complete my studies in Germany. I was offered the position of an assistant in a castle which had been transformed into a junior college. It was one of the most exclusive high schools in Germany where only the children of aristocratic and wealthy families went. I was heading towards the unknown and I was somewhat fearful but I thought: "I can always love." With this I departed.

The young people who attended this school (they ranged in age from thirteen to eighteen) came from very wealthy families. They had everything they wanted, but there were countless cases of alcohol and drug abuse; permissiveness and moral emptiness abounded.

Even some of the teachers and the assistants had a very relaxed attitude about these things. Behind it all I discovered families that were in pieces, young people without guidance, parents who sent money and gifts from all over the world but who never once appeared at the school. Above all there was a sense of infinite loneliness.

I started by trying to make friends with the group of boys

entrusted to me. They were amazed to see me sit down with them in front of the TV set because no other assistant had ever done it. I wanted to love all of them. So I talked, I kidded and I laughed with them, especially with those who were most alone, and left out. They couldn't believe the way I acted, but I felt that it was Jesus urging me to do it.

I realized that many divisions existed among them. What could I do about it? I resolved the problem with a big box of spaghetti. I invited them all to come to dinner at my place. It turned out to be a game in which everyone helped by looking for missing cutlery and plates or washing the pots.

As they left that evening many stopped to say: "This was the nicest evening of my life. What was new was the harmony among us all."

Monica, the cleaning lady, was treated with disdain. Whenever something was missing from the rooms she was immediately blamed. She used to greet me respectfully but just a smile back on my part was not enough.

One morning I prepared some coffee and cake and invited her to come in. At first she refused. Then she decided to enter, drank her coffee and, thanking me, left. I did the same on other mornings as well. One day, bursting into tears, she said, "My husband always beats me, my children give me all kinds of trouble and I have to stoop every day to cleaning bathrooms. That very morning before you invited me in for coffee I had already decided to end it all. But since then something has always stopped me."

Our friendship grew. She told me she was a Catholic. We decided to try and live some of the words of the gospel. Then we told one another how it went. Her relationships at home started to change for the better. Peace returned. Now the tears that fell from her eyes were tears of joy.

One Sunday I found Johannes alone. He spoke very little in French class. I invited him to come for coffee. We prepared it together and he began to tell me his story: abandoned as a child he was brought to live with his grandparents a block away from his mother who was living with another man. He suffered terribly over this and I with him. I let him get everything off his chest. Actually I couldn't think of a thing to say. In the end he looked up at me. He was peaceful and smiling. "Thank you," he said.

I knew he liked water polo and I had the keys to the pool. "Shall we go and play?" He went running for his things.

Michael had not seen his father for years and now his mother was about to leave him too. I knew she was coming for the Easter dance but I didn't know what to do. I asked Jesus to give me an idea. Of course! When she arrives she'll have to get changed for the dance. "Here are the keys to my apartment," I told her as soon as she arrived. "I have prepared some tea for you, too. You'll find everything you need." And off I went.

I saw her later that evening and I knew she had talked with her son. She stopped me and said, "I understand now that I have to love my son. It became clear to me seeing how much Michael loves you after knowing you for such a short time and by seeing how much you care for him."

One evening I came in late from a meeting and I didn't realize that one of the boys was not there. The next day I was told that Peter had gone home. His father shot himself after his company went bankrupt.

This too was a great suffering. I didn't know what to do. He lived too far away for me to go personally but I couldn't just sit there. After a long search I located his address and his phone number. I prepared a telegram assuring him that he was not alone.

The next day the phone rang. It was Peter. "No one ever showed so much love for me before." Soon he returned and our friendship continued to grow. I told him about myself, my life. He wanted to try and live the same way. I found out that he liked to go off-roading, and that his father used to take him often. So off we went in my car over the hills and fields of the area. The joy I saw in his eyes helped calm my fears.

Near the end of my stay in Germany I saw how the words of Jesus came true: "Give and you will be given." My room was full of things that had been lent to me or given. It was all love that was being returned. I had two television sets, one black and white and one color, I had plants, books, magazines, posters, plates and cutlery. Then the boys discovered that I played the guitar. At one point I had "only" five beautiful guitars to play. Too bad I didn't have ten hands.

The day of my departure approached. I decided to buy little presents for all of them and for the other assistants as well. The directors offered me a permanent position but I knew that the will of God for me was another. At a meeting in the cafeteria three hundred people—teachers, students and assistants—expressed their thanks with a long applause. Inside, however, I thanked Jesus because I knew that he had been the one to touch their hearts.

On the train heading home I thought over the months spent at the school and I was overwhelmed by a sense of gratitude to Jesus. "Thank you for all that you did. I'm leaving a piece of my heart there; but now, going back to Italy, my heart still wants to beat."

Thus Tony concluded—simply and without particular emphasis. A moment of silence and then a long applause rose up from every corner of the room. Everyone felt that that heart really still did want to beat, even if it costs his very life.

He stood there somewhat confused, moved and tired after the effort made to concentrate. He wanted to give just the essential and he ended up giving all of himself.

Next, Mass: a moment of great participation in which all, illuminated by the love they have given and received, sensed something and remained touched. Today's gospel brings us to Tabor and the transfiguration. Jesus is present and he is there for everyone. His desire is to enter and abide in people's hearts and it doesn't matter to him if this takes place in an ex-warehouse where there are neither windows nor paintings, nor drawings of saints on the walls.

There might be some budding saints however: especially there on the stage among the young people singing the alleluia, or even in the audience, someone who came reluctantly to Loppiano and who now finds himself or herself moved by the love of God who speaks within: a God who is so different from the one known until now. Some give in immediately, others try to resist for fear of being taken in. But the Voice within calls out ever more loudly: "Lazarus, come out. . ."

Meetings

Choosing God

Another Sunday, another round of guests. In the early afternoon I happened upon a group of people in their fifties. One of them asked for some information. He introduced himself and I reciprocated briefly. When I said that I lived in Loppiano they all looked at me with particular interest. Perhaps it hadn't occurred to them that Loppiano was home to both young and old.

They were from the southern part of Italy and they shared their comments on what they had seen that morning. I saw myself in them, the way I was at that age, and I observed them in silence. At a certain point, however, it came out that one of them worked as a director of a bank. "Which one?" I asked, raising my head. "As Treasury Inspector I was constantly involved with banks for at least thirty years." An intense dialogue began and I started to tell them about my spiritual adventure.

Another one of the group stated that he was an ophthalmologist. Once again I entered the conversation. "Do you know Dr. Pannarale? He operated on me twenty years ago." "Was it a detached retina?" he inquired. "Exactly that. He saved my eye after two previous operations had failed. It took five months to recover but, I must confess, they were five months of grace."

Now they were not only staring at me but their eyes were popping out of their heads. And there I stood smiling.

A third person said that he was the director of a certain state agency which was going through a serious financial crisis. I knew about that as well and so our conversation took off as if we'd known one another for years.

It wasn't difficult therefore for me to share with them the fact that one day I too had chosen God as they had heard spoken of during the morning program in the hall. My confession continued: "I completely lost the use of one eye but I can see pretty clearly what I need to. I also lost my wife but the love of the Focolare community has surrounded me in such a way that I never felt that I was a widower, nor alone. Then, seeing that my two daughters no longer needed me, I entered one of our men's communities at the age of seventy-three, first in Rome and now here."

I had said enough to overturn all their mental categories. We went outside for a walk and stopped for coffee. Three of them bought my autobiography *Lazarus, Come Out* and asked me to sign it.

"Gladly," I replied and headed for a quiet corner to collect my thoughts. I wrote a personal note for each of them.

One by one they opened their books and read my words. First one, then the other and then the third embraced me warmly.

"They come from the south," I thought, "and I understand them. I feel like a southerner myself."

To build together

The afternoon brought further encounters. This time I found myself with a group from Verona. They asked if they could visit the woodworking shop and the ceramics center. They asked about the cultivation of the fields. I went along with them and explained everything we were seeing.

When the tour was over one of them exclaimed in surprise, "So these young people study and work and do all kinds of jobs!"

"Certainly they do! 'If anyone is unwilling to work, neither should that one eat' (2 Thes 3:10). This school in Loppiano is not like a university you go to earn a degree. It is a school of life in which each person learns those basic values which will make of him or her a 'new person.'

"Actually," I concluded, "work and studies are not seen as an end in themselves, but rather as a means of fulfilling oneself in mutual understanding and therefore in the closest solidarity. All of this is a concrete demonstration that it is possible to build a society based on higher values than those we see around us today. We are not born brothers and sisters; it's a process."

I looked around at the thoughtful expressions on the faces of the people listening to me. I feared I had not explained myself too well. Seeing that they remained silent I thought of telling a well-known story that illustrates the meaning of work. Since they said they didn't know it I began:

A man was walking along a country road, carefully observing all that he saw. He came upon a group of laborers hammering a pile of stones with a sledge hammer. Curious as to their task he approached one of them.

"What are you doing?"

"Can't you see I'm breaking up these rocks!"

The man wasn't satisfied with this answer and he approached a second worker. "What are you doing?"

"Well, I'm earning a living for my wife and children."

Our traveller observed that this answer already contained a more humanitarian vision, but he still wasn't completely satisfied so he approached the third.

"What are you doing?"

This worker looked up, smiled warmly and replied:

"My dear sir, we are building the Cathedral!"

I finished. Any further comments would have been superfluous. My friends were happy and satisfied.

One of them observed: "Here you are reviving a type of competition that flourished between our medieval cities, even among the people of the working class. They were constantly trying to excel in creating things that were more beautiful and more noble."

"The most important thing however," another interjected, "is that plural form—'we are building'; that effort to work together to build something that will ennoble the whole city."

All approved and a "how very beautiful" was heard among the crowd.

"Of course," said another, "it really is beautiful. Unfortunately for us, what 'ennobles' a city today is having a good football team."

Laughter broke out and subsided immediately. Another person, a history professor, brought up the fact that the competition to excel that existed between the different cities was so fierce that it sometimes even led to war. "Today," he continued, "this no longer happens. A war between Florence and Pisa is inconceivable. Even a war between European nations is unthinkable. Peace is breaking out now. The day will soon come in which all arms will be laid down and peace will finally reign among us.

A lively discussion was under way. I let everyone express their thoughts and then I felt I had to add something. "And when we reach this point, which would already be quite an accomplishment, will we be happy? Will it be enough for us just to lead a tranquil but rather vegetative existence: eating, drinking and sleeping? No, this will not be enough for us! Man does not live on bread alone. A society of people is called to be something more than an army of hard-working and well-organized ants."

My friends looked at me and smiled, nodding their heads in agreement. They were all good Catholics, but perhaps a discourse as clear as this one, stated quite matter-of-factly while walking along a country road, might be news to them.

Hoping against all hope

Having paused over coffee and conversation we then had to hurry back to the hall for the afternoon program. It included songs and experiences of life shared by young people coming from all over the world. The audience admired the song offered by some young women from Korea. A husband and wife shared about their relationship with their five children. A concluding mime prepared by a group of children added a note of joyful enthusiasm.

The day was concluding. Now came the moment when those who wished could go up on stage and offer their impressions of the day. No one moved. People looked at one another as if to say, "Why don't you go?" But still they hesitated. Finally a courageous young woman went up to say that she would have never imagined that there existed in the world a model of society such as she witnessed here. She was very enthusiastic and declared that she would be back.

Anyone else?

Seconds passed and a man went up to say more or less the same thing. He was on his way down the steps when another person stood waiting for his turn. Impression slips were passed out so that everyone had a chance to offer their comments.

The musical group went back up on stage to conclude the program with a song and bid farewell to the guests. I was struck by the vigorous yet gentle fullness of the song which I heard that day for the first time. The words were taken from a passage of the gospel and they underscored the meaning of this encounter:

We have given up everything for you, O Lord
In return, we ask, what will we receive?
We have left our families for you, O Lord
Having done all this, we ask what will we receive?

Looked upon by your love,
We have followed your call
Not wanting anything more,
And you have drawn us closer, closer to you.

"Blessed are you! Blessed are you! Blessed are you!
Because yours is the kingdom.
You will gain much more upon this earth
And you'll gain life for all eternity.

You will perform works greater than mine.
I will live in you. You will live in me."

Applause thundered forth. The day was over but the people were reluctant to get up and go. So was I. One's soul had been opened up onto a vision of a life without end, a life too great to be grasped in its full dimension, too beautiful, it seemed, to be true. And yet one can always hope against all hope.

Utopia

The future city

The people all left. Some would have to travel all night. I started out for home and then turned back and went to the reception area where people were collecting the impression slips left by the visitors. I wanted to see what they had written so as to be sure that it all wasn't just a dream.

I picked up a pile of them and leafed through it to choose the most meaningful ones. The form also included a space for the person to write his or her age and I have included it here in parentheses.

I just recently married. If I have the grace to have a child I would like to see him or her live in a world modelled on Loppiano (24).

Loppiano: a little paradise on earth (58).

Throughout this whole day I felt my heart cry for joy (26).

Even though I am a nun I have been very enriched with love for my neighbor and God (45).

Here you don't have to close your eyes to dream (19).

I would just like to thank you for existing in this world (43).

Before coming my mind was full of doubts and why's. I'm leaving now with my heart full of your love and your smiles (43).

As I listened to you I was constantly trying to make a comparison between your way of life and the Marxist approach, especially when you spoke about a communion of goods. But you are not on the attack! What surprises me is this: there is no class struggle and yet you have a very revolutionary thrust. I want to keep in touch (24).

Now I know you don't have to die to experience paradise (22).

I am convinced now that the much-awaited unity of peoples is not just a dream (24).

I was struck by the joy of "feeling young" in spite of my age (68).

Listening to you and watching you this morning I experienced a new, deep joy that I couldn't identify. Then, during Mass, your songs and the recitation of the story of the Transfiguration opened my eyes (26).

What could I add: these statements, as simple as they were, spoke eloquently.

Thousands of visitors have come to Loppiano since its founding in 1964 and their impressions would all fit into the spectrum reported above.

A priest of a religious order, who has known the Focolare for many years, confided to me that he saw our little city as the reflection of the heavenly Jerusalem spoken of in the Book of Revelation. He recited the passage by memory:

"I saw the holy city, a new Jerusalem, coming down out of heaven from God, prepared as a bride adorned for her husband. . . I saw no temple in the city, for its temple is the Lord God almighty and the Lamb" (Rev 21:2, 22).

What a wonderful image! Therefore our little city which has neither cathedral nor abbey and yet reflects something of that divine splendor—because "The Lamb is its light"—could be seen as the prophetic image of the future city.

Is it a utopia? No! Not by chance, today, one dares to speak of a way toward a "social sanctity" to be reached not on an individual basis but collectively, that is, as a "mystical body." In actual fact it would be a matter of re-establishing on earth that first Christian community in which "the community of believers was of one heart and mind, and no one claimed that any of his possessions was his own, but they had everything in common" (Acts 4:32).

Lay people are at last realizing that inasmuch as they are baptized they participate in the mystery of the death and resurrection of Christ: and therefore all together they form the living Church, a missionary Church.

For them it is not a questions of one's race, or origin, language or political beliefs. What is essential is to give God all that he deserves: soul, mind and heart. All else has no importance for the purposes of the true life.

"For stern as death is love" (Sg 8:6). Herein lies true liberation.

Jesus, Jesus of Nazareth, you who live in our midst, let this always be true. Weren't you the one who taught us to pray that it might be "on earth as it is in heaven."

We are trying. But you, Jesus, continue to sustain us as we continue to do our part.

Someone pays

In the meantime someone is paying so the future might quickly become the present.

The other day—December 18, 1983—at just twenty-five years of age Tony Daga suddenly died—that young man, my dear friend whose story I shared with you already.

I had seen him just a few hours before. He had seemed somewhat paler than usual. But then when I saw him stretched out on a bed I couldn't help crying out within me, "No! . . . no!"

It was only when someone whispered, "He was an angel and the Lord wanted him in paradise" that I could lift my eyes and dry my tears.

Going back home I read over some of Tony's poems. In them I found such profound meaning that I wanted to share them with others.

Humility

Humility,
you realize what it is
when you must accept it
and you can't make it.

Humility,
which means faithfulness
to that insignificant thing
you are doing . . .
as if it were the last one,
and because it is the last one.

Humility,
means being cut to the quick,
accepting to not exist
and remaining in the game.

Humility,
to stay when you would like to go;
to fail when you would like to win;
to humble yourself when you would like to emerge.

Humility,
it is that golden thread which gives life
both to the present
and to the future. . .

Even if you cannot see,
or hear,
child on the road of Wisdom,
wait.

The Cross

Like a constant drop
that intends to penetrate a rock

firmly repeating
"Make room, let me in."

If I say yes,
with no "ifs" or "buts,"
I discover I can truly
love that drop of water
and I await only
the moment of its fall.

It's strange,
because naturally it would be unusual,
and yet you realize
that the more suffering penetrates
the more Love grows. . .
And you live . . . *you live.*

The cross . . .
is the drop from Heaven,
an offering of His infinite Love.

I read the verses over and over and thought of Father Mondrone who wrote a series of biographies on personalities of our times (including Igino Giordani) entitled: *There are still Saints.* Why couldn't someone collect other biographies and call it: *There are still Angels.*

I think that there are some young people who do not need to reach their golden years to be able to completely open up to the Love of God. Others—alas poor me!—try to resist the utterance of that drop which insistently repeats: "Make room, let me in!"

My Eightieth Birthday

We elderly

The years pass by. Strength—along with sight, hearing and other faculties—diminishes in efficiency. And yet we elderly still find hovering within us that touch of pride that makes it hard for us to ask for help in spite of the other's readiness to give it.

This morning for example I found myself faced with a small problem and I wasn't sure if I should try to solve it myself or if I should ask for the help of my friends in the focolare household. All of a sudden the episode of the Last Supper came to my mind. I pictured Jesus who, in order to set an example, washed his disciples' feet.

They, speechless, allowed him to do it. When Jesus got to Peter, however, that disciple vigorously opposed such a thing. "Lord, you shall never wash my feet!" he exclaimed. Jesus merely replied, "Then you shall have no share in my heritage."

Upon hearing this Peter shook himself, opened his eyes and realized what was happening. "Lord, then not only my feet, but my hands and head as well" (Jn 13:8-9).

Oh Peter. If I had been around in those days I would have thrown my arms around your neck saying, "Thank you Peter. You are just like all of us!"

What more could Jesus have done to help us understand that we must help one another? How ever will we make it to follow him, as stubborn and proud as we are, even in our old age?

Actor and spectator

Here I am then with all my pride and limitations. Tomorrow, December 4, 1984, I will be eighty years old. My knees shake when I go down the stairs, my hand shakes when I pour milk into my cup. Poor me! I really am quite a wreck. A walking wreck.

But saying this word "wreck" makes me think of how I felt after that long illness of so many years ago. During those five months of recuperation, punctuated by repeated operations on my eyes and the threat of blindness, I had made it to stay on the crest of the wave, morally and spiritually. I even made it to give new courage and hope to those visitors who came with downcast expressions.

But when I finally got home and realized that with the only eye left I could just barely see I fell into a deep crisis. On that occasion it was my guardian angel in the form of a very dear friend who brought me back up to the surface.

He wanted to know how I was and I unloaded onto him all my bitterness. "I just can't make it any more, Julius," I lamented. "This is it for me. My left eye is gone. The right one should get a little better but I can barely make things out. I'm a wreck, a total wreck!"

My friend, who knew me quite well, answered me with the courage that comes from love. "So you feel like a wreck, do you? Well you are a wreck. And what difference does it make? Even Jesus hanging on the cross had reduced himself to just such a state. What counts now is that you 'commend' this wreck into the hands of the Father and allow Him to use you as He wants. Then life will become a wonderful adventure in which you will be both actor and spectator at the same time."

And I must confess that's just what happened. And I hope it will stay this way: good for nothing, me; good for everything, Him.

A celebration for everyone

I always kept my birthday a secret. On the other hand it fell at a time when we all usually went to Rome from Loppiano for our annual retreat. This year the meeting was moved to another date and so here we all were in Loppiano. My friend Mino discovered my secret and, without saying anything to me, went around telling everyone that it was Matthew's eightieth birthday.

My suspicions were aroused when many people passing me by on the road greeted me with uncharacteristic warmth and mysterious glee. One person even slowed down the car he was driving to wave at me. Others winked knowingly as if to say, "Do you know?"

"Know what?"

It didn't take long to discover: they wanted to throw a party for me. But not just any old party. They wanted to invite everyone of the community and hold it in our meeting hall.

When I found that out I began to feel ill at ease. That they might want to have a little party was certainly understandable but I didn't want to be the center of attention. What had I done that was bad? Nothing really. And that was good? Nothing unfortunately. So the celebration should be for them not for me I reasoned. I had to concede that the only eighty-year-old Focolarino available at the moment was me, but. . .

No "buts" about it! I was going to have to co-operate.

And yet I was burdened inside. I started looking for Fr. Mario who normally hears my confession because I wanted to make a complete examination of conscience with him. He was nowhere to be found.

I poured out my soul to a friend. As I was speaking an idea made its way into my head. "If we are going to go ahead with this celebration," I said, "I think we should make it everyone's celebration, not dedicated just to me, but to all the elderly around us even if they are not part of this community."

He smiled and agreed. He listed a few names and I consented reminding him not to forget Lydia, the mother of one of the Focolarini, who is three years my senior, an unforgettable lady!

That child. . .

I headed out early the next morning for the usual visit to my great Friend who awaits me silently in the tabernacle of our little chapel. My customary serenity was overshadowed by the thought of the celebration to take place that evening.

I stopped at the bottom of a little hill in the road. Something was definitely wrong, out of kilter. "I have only one Spouse on earth, Jesus crucified and forsaken," Chiara had once written. And I had followed her in this choice. But where was that Jesus now? Here, celebration was in the air.

It didn't take long for the answer to come. That Jesus is within me in the suffering I experience at the thought that a party is about to be held to honor a poor fellow who reached this age through no personal merit, rather thanks to God's grace alone. Everything I am or I have was given to me. . . It should be me rather to get down on my knees and kiss the ground in thanksgiving to God and ask for his mercy!

But following the suffering there is light. All of a sudden I discovered that yes, I could take part in the celebration in the full awareness that I was like the man who had made friends using another's wealth (cf. Lk 16:1-8). I too could offer praise for these eighty years of mine.

Peace returned and I entered the chapel.

A ray of light crowned the tabernacle. The rest of the room lay in darkness. I chose a seat and recovered my breath as I attempted to recollect myself in the presence of the Friend who is always there awaiting me. "I'm here, Jesus," I murmured as I do every morning.

No reply came. That was to be expected. But I am certain that when my time comes he will come close by and whisper with all his love, "I'm here, Matthew."

I sat at length in silence. Peace filled my soul. I felt poor and weak but desirous of His Love. I was aware of my limitations but He consoled me as usual: "Don't worry," he seemed to say, "I know you, you're the impulsive type. But just go ahead like this."

Tranquil once again I moved towards the exit and stopped in front of an icon of Our Lady which was hung to the right of the altar a few weeks ago. I wanted to get a better look but it was too dark in the room and I could barely make it out. I switched on the lights and studied this completely new Mary with joy and surprise.

It was the Icon of Vladimir, depicting maternal tenderness. The work of an unknown artist, it was brought from Constantinople to Russia in 1131. It was not the usual image of a young woman dressed in white with a blue sash around her waist and her feet resting on a cloud. No, this depicted an adult mother holding a child in her arms. His, however, are not baby-like features. He is a little boy who, with his cheek against his mothers, reaches forward to kiss her. There is just the hint of a smile on her lips. No, it is not a smile. If you look closely you realize that it is more an expression of intense sadness. The words of old Simeon seem branded on her heart: "And you yourself shall be pierced with a sword" (Lk 2:35). Perhaps she foresaw the suffering of Calvary: and now she holds this son in her arms in an attitude of reverence mixed with anguish.

I stood rooted there, intent upon the image of the Child with his serious expression and his arms flung around his mother. He seemed to be clinging to her. One of his hands in fact appears from behind her neck. Yes, she is holding him but in reality he has her tightly in his arms, imploring her.

How I understand him! That child, O Lord, is me!

A beat of the heart, a burning sensation in my eyes . . . and the tears, sweet tears began to flow.

Thank you Jesus. I haven't cried like this in a long time.

One Big Family

Poor me

Late that afternoon my daughter Chiaretta arrived from Rome with her husband Michele and their twenty-year-old son Francesco.

We all ate together in the focolare center and everything went along in such a normal manner that they were surprised.

At the end of the meal I explained that there was going to be a celebration, but not here. It would take place in a small meeting hall nearby and, as a matter of fact, we had to leave right away because it was getting late.

It took only a few minutes to get there. As we walked in the main door applause broke out from the two hundred people crowding the room. I felt more bewildered than moved.

"Up to the front, up to front," voices nearby urged. And we slowly made our way to the front row.

Finally we took our seats and calm returned. Bob, our young MC, gave the official welcome and invited on stage those who had prepared something for the evening's celebration.

One after the other, groups of young people introduced themselves and offered a little bit of everything: a Brazilian dance, the Ave Maria sung by the Argentineans, an African sing-a-long, a Korean song and even—this one I really didn't expect—a ballad sung in verses and dedicated to me. They had come up with it just a few hours before and now here they were singing it to me. What rascals! They had even discovered my real name! Listen to this:

To Matthew

Alceste Silvi
a man fine and true
worked in the Treasury
as well as one can do.

But then came the day
to the Mariapolis he went
and midst angelic song
a total change he sensed.

Now his life was different
he also changed his name
Matthew Silvan he would be
And naught would be the same.

With a smile on his face
he went on his way
and loved every neighbor
he encountered each day

But that was not all
because God had a plan
and called him to leave all
and follow him and then

It was in the Focolare,
there was his place
with Light and with Love
he continued his race.

And now Happy Birthday
Loppiano will sing
to Matthew Silvan
and our thank you we bring.

But may all the glory
be God's on this day
who gave you these years
to grow in sanctity.

"Those rascals, those rascals," I thought to myself. How could they tease a poor old fellow, and especially on his birthday!

But they were all happily laughing. What could I do? I wanted to cry out, "That's it, that's enough!" but it would have served no purpose.

By now everyone was applauding. Well, that was to be expected. I wondered what my family was thinking. I couldn't help but notice their astonished expressions. It was all quite different from what they—accustomed as they were to a university environment—expected. My grandson Francesco, on the other hand, was enjoying it immensely. Everyone understood that if we could celebrate and play together in such a manner it was because we were all one big family.

The celebration continued. The members of the musical group Gen Rosso climbed up on stage and sang a song that began with the words, "Today in my heart I have so much joy. . ."Applause followed and then, finally, silence.

Never in descent, only ascent

Bob, our MC, came over and whispered, "Matthew, this is your moment to say something of your life experience, both for the young and the old who are here."

I sat in silence for another moment or two trying to come up with an idea that would be in tune with the atmosphere of the celebration. I rose to my feet and began my greetings. Applause broke out and I used those valuable seconds to put my thoughts together.

"Today in my heart I have so much joy is what we sang together now, but actually in my head I have much confusion. However we are all one family and now I'll let you in on what is passing through my mind. This morning, while you were preparing this celebration, I couldn't help asking myself if it was right to allow it to happen because the credit certainly doesn't go to me if I managed to live to be eighty years of age .

"Then I thought about it further and I became aware of all my faults and failures, both past and present and that procured me enough suffering to be able to stand first of all before God whom I was visiting in the tabernacle.

"And He seemed to respond almost immediately saying, 'Don't fret about your shortcomings. I already know what you are like. You've even tried to storm my Kingdom by asking me over and over again to send you trials. And I granted your request. Now you are here with me so be at peace and accept yourself as you are. If your friends want to have a celebration, enjoy it with them, but keep your heart fixed on the reality that you know so well, so as not to go off the track.'

"So here I am my friends. I don't want to make a long speech. For those of us who live here in Loppiano we already have a certain understanding about many things. We well know, for example, that in the journey that lies ahead, if we remain faithful to Christ, then the journey is never a descent toward the tomb. Rather it is an ascent toward heaven. . .

"Our journey is one toward God as we try to acquire anew, inasmuch as is possible, the innocence of children. Our way of acquiring this innocence is by detaching ourselves, a little at a time, from all that is not essential, abandoning all our little skirmishes and shedding the dust we collected along the way. We should reach the point of having but a few words to say, the essential ones which are the fruit of wisdom. And these, too, even when expressed only through a smile, will have to express only one thing: Love.

"Suffering will always be with us, moments of darkness, too. But we know that it has a name. All our pain has meaning if it is united to that of Jesus when the lance pierced his side. We cannot avoid it and we cannot let it stop us. We must go beyond the wound and return to the light, or better, smile because the Risen Lord is with us.

"Thank you all very much!"

I Love These "Golden Years"

The one who loves, knows God

Applause broke out. I now turned to those in the audience who were not part of the community of Loppiano:

"Some of you might think that old age is synonymous with ailments and loneliness. I would like to inform you that even if often there might be no cure for a physical illness except the relief that a good doctor might be able to offer, for the loneliness that you might experience even in the midst of a busy city, there is a cure. There is a friend, that Jesus whom I referred to not long ago, is always near at hand, speaking to us with words of love.

"You might not know this Jesus very well. And yet his presence is there within you, he is the voice of your conscience. Listen to him, I implore you, listen to him! I am speaking to you like a brother. Become friends with those who already know him!

"Perhaps some of you might have had a certain prejudice regarding religious matters. But my dear friends, open your eyes. This poor, tormented earth is not the only existing reality. There exists also a heaven which goes on forever. Where does the infinite end? Don't you experience in this question which knows no answer, the sense of mystery, the intuition of God?

"It's true that no one has seen God. St. John the apostle admits this but he also adds that 'If we love one another, God dwells in us and his love is brought to perfection in us' (1 Jn 4:12).

"The one who loves, therefore, has knowledge of God even if he or she doesn't know it, because 'God is love.' As for myself I have experienced that the one who loves lives in fullness, not the one who waits to be loved by the others.

"Very often, immersed as we are in the daily events of the

world, we suffer for today's situation and worry about tomorrow's. Jesus' words to us are: 'Today has troubles enough of its own' (Mt 6:34). This means that we should live the present moment with fullness, without worrying about what the future might bring. After all I know that I could die this very night.

"Let us try to do all things well as if it were the last thing we were going to do. This will guarantee us the peace that Jesus promised to those who entrust themselves to him.

"Dear friends, I'm not even sure where I'm finding the courage to talk to you so openly. Some of you might even think that I am just a poor dreamer, that I really haven't understood anything of what life is all about. If you only knew what I've been through, in war and in peace. But I don't want to talk to you about things I read about in books, but rather about what I found in the gospel, what I heard, understood and transformed into life. Here it is, expressed in concrete facts, my life today. I will let you be the judge.

"I lost the use of one eye and am partially blind in the other but I see very clearly what is essential: 'My night knows no darkness.'

"I have little money in my pockets and yet I do not feel I am poor.

"I wash the dishes every day at home, but this is all part of the game of love.

"I lost my wife, the person most dear to me on earth but I do not feel alone. My natural family was immediately replaced by a 'supernatural' family: the focolare center where I live, love and feel that I am loved.

"In closing let me say that I have reached eighty years of age, but I feel like I was born yesterday. Everything fills me with a sense of wonder.This morning, looking into the eyes of a baby in its cradle I had the impression that I was discovering the beauty of creation for the first time.

"What more can I say. Yes, this. I love these golden years and I adore that God who has granted them to me!"

Interval

Applause broke out again. Bob came up to me and whispered that the cake was arriving.

They had really thought of everything.

A voice cried, "Bravo, Valentino!" and the artist-cook-pastry chef smiled good-naturedly.

It wasn't just one cake but many, offered on trays that went up and down the rows. One appeared before me with a very big candle on top.

"This candle counts for eighty," I was told.

I blew out the flame and my daughter helped cut the cake and pass it out. It was all happily devoured. Once again it was Bob whispering at my side: "Matthew do you remember that we said we would finish with you reading one of your poems? That will end the evening well."

"Yes, I remember, I brought it with me." And yet I remained seated.

Now I would have to read the poem. Actually it wasn't really a poem, it was more like a collection of verses that had come to me in different moments that I then put together. I was still perplexed. I was afraid that my recitation would not go with the atmosphere of celebration and the sweet smell of birthday cake that had meanwhile filled the hall. But there was no way out.

I got up and tried to smile. Someone must have sensed my embarrassment so an applause of encouragement sprang up. I tried to think of something to say that would prepare the audience for my piece.

My soul magnifies the Lord

"Dear friends, here I am again. This will be the last number in this evening's performance. Perhaps it's not what you're expecting. Just a few moments ago you heard how these friends of mine teased me by singing a little poem. Well I too have a little poem, but it's a serious one. No song will be sung except the song that might spring forth from the silence of one's heart.

"Please don't expect a creative masterpiece from me. I spent my life in matters of finance and I have always been convinced that two plus two makes four. Fortunately, at a certain point in my life, having shed the robes of the Inspector General of the Treasury, I understood that it is much more beautiful if one can reach the point that through the presence of Love two plus two makes five. Let those who have ears understand.

"So here I am. Yes, I have even dared to attempt poetry. In vain I searched for the most searing and beautiful words that I knew: nothing was able to express the fullness that flows out from a heart that is in love with Love. But since I knew that Jesus does not look down on the words of the poor, I turned to him with my faltering phrases:

Thank you Lord, thank you
for that day many years ago
when you reduced me to nothing
to lead me back to your will.

Thank you for having called me
to live in your city
and letting me see
the radiant dawn of your civilization.

Thank you for having stolen my heart
and perhaps even my mind:
you took it all for yourself
and reduced me to nothing.

And I, as wretched as I am, still dare to sing:
my soul magnifies the Lord,
and my spirit exults in You
my Truth, my Savior.

Why—tell me—did you want

to use me, a poor tax collector?
You looked at me, touched me,
took me by hand.

Here I am now, in love with everything
with heaven and with the earth
with the rain and the sun
with Your peace and Your war.

Now in me suffering
evolves into a smile
And everything on the earth
is a prelude to paradise.

There is a Woman, up there, clothed in the sun
Virgin, Mother, all of God.
Amidst the angels and saints encircled around her
there is Teresa*, my angel!

Let me join them, Lord!
Let me step over the threshold of suffering
and then lose myself, happily, in You,
dear, sublime, infinite. . .

eternal Love."

---

* Author's deceased wife.